Practical Performance Improvement

Practical Performance Improvement

How to Be an Exceptional People Manager

Rod Matthews

BEP BUSINESS EXPERT PRESS

Practical Performance Improvement: How to Be an Exceptional People Manager
Copyright © Business Expert Press, LLC, 2018.

First published in 2018 by
Business Expert Press, LLC
222 East 46th Street, New York, NY 10017
www.businessexpertpress.com

ISBN-13: 978-1-94819-804-2 (paperback)
ISBN-13: 978-1-94819-805-9 (e-book)

Business Expert Press Human Resource Management and Organizational Behavior Collection

Collection ISSN: 1946-5637 (print)
Collection ISSN: 1946-5645 (electronic)

Cover and interior design by S4Carlisle Publishing Services Private Ltd., Chennai, India

First edition: 2018

10 9 8 7 6 5 4 3 2 1

Printed in the United States of America.

Abstract

Anyone who is responsible for the supervision and performance of a team in an organization will appreciate the practical management strategies outlined in this book. In a refreshing, humorous, and engaging approach, it aims to reduce the stress associated with the leadership of a team of people and improve the likelihood that things get done right, the first time. Written by Rod Matthews, the Australian facilitator and presenter often referred to as "the best trainer in Australia," it provides great insight and practical exercises on how to be an exceptional manager and team leader. In a step-by-step approach, it will help you be better at coaching and developing team members, setting direction for your team, and enhancing performance and engagement. A must read for all first-time managers/team leaders who want to get the best out of their team.

Keywords

coaching team members, developing team members, engagement, leadership, management, managing poor performance, performance, setting direction, supervision, team

Contents

How to Get the Most Out of This Book.......................................*ix*

Acknowledgments..*xi*

Chapter 1   But It's Not My Job . . . It's Theirs!.........................1

Chapter 2   How to Objectively Analyze the
            Performance of Your Team...................................13

Chapter 3   Tactics to Improve Performance..........................25

Chapter 4   Coaching...31

Chapter 5   Developing...49

Chapter 6   Counseling...67

Chapter 7   Reassigning..91

Chapter 8   Establishing a Direction....................................99

Chapter 9   Don't Be a Turkey...107

Bibliography...*111*

About the Author...*113*

Index..*115*

How to Get the Most Out of This Book

Impact Human Performance Technologies has designed this and all of our books with the following saying in mind . . .

> *I hear and I forget,*
> *I see and I remember,*
> *I do and I understand!*

Our books are best read with a pencil in hand ready to take part in practical activities, exercises, and to record your thoughts, feelings, and experiences. In order to get the most out of this book, please be prepared to participate, record, and reflect as well as read.

The aim of our books is to provide you with lots of tips, tools, and techniques that you can actually use to leverage your and others' success.

There are a variety of ways you can use our books. For example:

- **Self-paced learning**
  The books are put together in a way that will allow you or work colleagues to complete the learning at their own pace.
- **To form part of training sessions or workshops**
  Please feel free to copy the material in this book to form part of your training sessions or workshops. What we ask is that you reference the material with:
  "© 2003 Rod Matthews, Impact Human Performance Technologies Pty Ltd."
- **As a resource in your organization's learning center**
  Together, all of the Impact books form an excellent library for any business interested in investing in their workforce or for any individual interested in investing in their own education.

Acknowledgments

Most of what we know is the amalgamation of personal experience, conversations with others, and reading. With this in mind, it would be impossible to acknowledge every person who has truly contributed to this book.

Team members, course participants, work colleagues, friends, and family have all played a role in building the book that you hold in your hands.

There are of course some people in particular that I must mention.

Family

My wife and best friend, Margaret. Thank you for all your love, support, and honesty. To my boys Liam and Riley, thank you for putting all the corporate stuff into perspective and wrestling with dad when needed a break.

Mentor

I have had the privilege owning a business with Robert Scanlon, who has been a role model for me on many levels. A large part of this book is as much Robert as it is me.

Book Reviewers

I have also had the privilege of getting to know some people through my work that I would count as my friends first and foremost. These people very kindly offered their time and considerable experience to provide me with some exceptional feedback. Their feedback has greatly increased the practicality and professionalism of this book. Thank you again:

- Kylie Sprott
- Steve Mitchinson
- Judith Burgess
- Toni Carroll
- Tracey Chapman-Marks
- Andrew Collier
- John Lambert

CHAPTER 1

But It's Not My Job . . . It's Theirs!

Are You Interested in Improving the Performance of Your Team Members?

Now I can understand at the beginning of a book such as this, that you might be thinking a number of different things to yourself. For example, you might be thinking:

"Thanks very much but I don't have the time. If you could see the thickness of my in-tray, if you could count the number of e-mails that are stacking up at this very moment, if you knew the number of people who are looking for me . . ."

Or you might be thinking . . .

> ". . . in your average organization 40 percent of work is rework! 40 percent of the work that the average person does in the average organization exists because something didn't go right the first time."

"Managing people is not rocket science. Either they can do the job or they can't. If they can, then great, they get paid. If they can't, then fine, they get sacked!"

Or you might be thinking . . .

"Listen, I've been around a bit. I've worked for a number of different organizations in a number of different capacities. What could this book possibly hold for me that I don't already know?"

No matter what you are thinking or feeling at this point, a number of things are true. This book that you hold in your hands and have chosen to read this far, is an excellent opportunity to do a number of things:

1. Look at what can be done to reduce the stress and frustration sometimes associated with dealing with team members who, at best, seem to be operating under a different agenda to yours, or at worst, seem to be keen to sabotage what it is you are trying to do.

2. Identify what it is that can be done to increase the likelihood that we get things right the first time. I remember reading an article where a consultant organization had done some research into organizations. The upshot of the article was that in your average organization 40 percent of work is rework! 40 percent of the work that the average person does in the average organization exists because something didn't go right the first time.

   Imagine how much extra time, money, energy, equipment, and brain space you would have on your hands if we could reduce this by 10 percent . . . even 5 percent!!!

3. This book also identifies what makes the difference! What makes the difference between a good manager of people and an *excellent* manager of people. An exceptional manager. A manager who clearly stands out head and shoulders above the rest.

   Think for a moment about all the managers you know of, who you would consider to be good or better. They could be people you work with as peers, people who you report to or people who report to you. If I asked you to take out the ones that just made "good" so you are left with the "very good" or better, the list would be shrinking.

   Now if I asked you to take out the ones that just made "very good," so you are left with only the "exceptional," chances are that there are very few people you can think of. And those that you do know stand out clearly. You probably even thought of them first.

So this book is an excellent opportunity to identify what it is that the "excellent" or "exceptional" manager does that the "good" doesn't. And how to do more of the excellent and less of the average.

Try this quick quiz . . .

Have You Ever . . .?

	Tick where appropriate
. . . been frustrated by underperforming team members?	
. . . found it difficult to manage people when you are understaffed?	
. . . wanted to reduce the amount of time you spend doing and redoing your team members' work?	
. . . wondered how the inspirational leader maintains a high level of commitment from their team while avoiding stress and burnout?	
. . . lost a high-performing team member because they were bored with the job?	
. . . resigned from a manager more than from a job, and want to make sure that good team members don't resign because of you?	
. . . been frustrated by people? For example: Their response when you have asked them to do something?	
. . . wondered what could be done to ensure your team members' morale remains high?	
. . . had to lead a team of people who were at different developmental levels and wanted to ensure that you were a consistent yet flexible leader?	
. . . considered how much easier your job would be as a leader when you have a highly competent and completely committed team working with you?	
. . . delivered feedback to a team member, which they took the wrong way?	
. . . wondered how you could free yourself up from day-to-day managing and increase the time you spend dealing with more strategic concerns?	

If you ticked any of the above then you're not Robinson Crusoe. Many team leaders and managers find themselves caught in a vicious cycle. Constantly busy with day-to-day operations, crises, and responding to deadlines. They are left with little or no time for tasks like planning, strategy, developing tactics, establishing systems, and developing the ability and motivation of their team.

Some Important Management Lessons

But first allow me to introduce myself. I left school, I guess like many people leave school, and that is with no clear understanding as to what I wanted to do after school. Fortunately, in some respects, I just got enough marks to go to university. So I went for a whole year and failed abysmally.

The reason I failed abysmally is because I found it very hard to fit any study into the hectic social calendar you have to keep when living on campus.

Two days before an exam or assignment due date, I would think to myself, "Ok Rod, if you're going to cram an entire terms worth of work, now is the time to start!" So I would set myself up. Books in reachable distance, mug of coffee on the boil, and I've popped a couple of "No-Doze" pills ("No-Doze" pills are 100 mg of caffeine. They are evil things! I'm sure truckies take them! You can feel the hairs on the back of your neck growing after a couple of these). A couple of these and you are going to stay awake for a good few hours yet!

Just as I was about to put pen to paper, there would be a knock at the door.

"Rod, we're going to the pub. What are you doing?"
"Give me two minutes. I'll be with you."

Now there were people at the university who were able to both kill brain cells on a nightly basis and pass with honors. I was not one of them. The idea at the end of the first year Uni was to get a job for a year and earn enough to put myself through second and third year.

I remember telling this to one of my tutors before I left. She responded with, "Well Rod, it was nice knowing you!"

I asked, "What do you mean?"

She replied, "90 percent of people who defer studies at the end of their first year do not come back. So . . . it was nice knowing you Rod!"

Obviously she had a little more experience with that than I did, . . . and she turned out to be right. I didn't go back. Instead, I found a job in a bank, got very used to having money in the wallet, and enjoyed an entry-level job that allowed me to continue with the party lifestyle.

Working the Farm

The bank is where I first came into contact with the concept of performance management. I was promoted up several levels in the bank and finally got to a management position. I can remember thinking to myself, "Fantastic! I'm going to be the best manager that ever lived."

What I decided to do was to meet the person I was replacing and ask a few questions about team direction, personalities, abilities etc. I phoned the person in question and we tried to find a common time in our diaries for a handover-type meeting.

The only time we could find was Friday afternoon, after lunch, on her last day in the job. Now, I don't know what it's like where you work, but in the bank in those days Friday afternoon was already an excuse to have an "executive lunch break." Add to that the fact that it was someone's last day and there was no argument. A liquid lunch it was!

Needless to say, the meeting was close to useless. The person I was meeting with was smashed and the meeting was interrupted every 10 minutes by someone coming in to say goodbye and hugs and kisses and promises to keep in touch . . . the whole tragedy.

> "No farmer in their right mind is going to leave a season's worth of work until the last 2 days in the season."

Toward the end of the meeting Robyn pulled out a manila folder and placed it on the desk in front of us.

"Rod," she said. "These are the team's performance appraisals. I've written them, I just haven't delivered them yet. So one of the first things you might want to do is to make a meeting with each team member and run through their appraisals."

Mr. Naïve, first-time manager, said, "Yeah. Great. Good opportunity to get to know the team!"

Anyone who has delivered performance appraisals before will know that it's tough enough when you have written them yourself. But to have to deliver what you did not write or observe is an added degree of difficulty.

The best way to describe the appraisal meetings is to call then "2 days of debate," 2 days of comments like:

"What does she mean here?"; "Why didn't she tell me that? I could have fixed it if it was that much of an issue."; "Why only a '3'? What do I have to do to get a '5'?"

Something I learned very quickly about management was that it is a year-round activity. Anyone who thinks they can leave the people bit of management until the last few days before the appraisal is due or the last few days before salary review is fooling themselves and setting themselves up for a lot of extra work, frustration, and wasted time.

Managing people, leading people (however, you may want to spell it) is a bit like working the farm. No farmer in their right mind is going to leave a season's worth of work until the last 2 days in the season. If they did, they would not be a farmer for long. The "excellent" farmers are out there every day—doing a little every day—working the farm every day.

And so it is with managing people: you need to "work the farm" a little every day.

It's not the forms and it's not the systems . . .

The bank and I eventually parted company and I went to work for a leading wholesaler and marketer of quality electronic products who also had a performance management system.

There were lots of complaints from managers about the performance management systems;

"What do I write here?"
"What do I do if . . .?"
"How do I know what to give them?"

The human resources department, being the proactive responsive little group that they were, decided that the system needed updating. Feedback was sought, focus groups where held, research was conducted, forms were redesigned, procedures changed, information simplified, and the new system was launched.

Six months later, the managers were still asking the same questions, unsure about the same things, and still concerned about the same issues.

What we learned there was that if performance management is a task that is 1-meter long, the forms, systems, and procedures will only contribute about 10 centimeters!

You could have the world's best, most objective, easy-to-use system ever designed and if the person using it is a complete loser, it won't work.

By the same token, you could have a blank piece of paper and a crayon, and if the person using that paper and crayon has some great interpersonal skills then performance management will be fine, thank you very much.

What makes the difference when it comes to managing people is the skills of the manager.

From the Outside Looking in . . .

There are both benefits and drawbacks of being a consultant. One of the drawbacks is that we are just above politicians and used car salesmen in the food chain. One of the benefits is that you get to work with a wide variety of organizations—variety of size, method of operation, market, industry, culture, etc. In working with the wide variety you start to be able to build an understanding as to what makes the difference when it comes to many things—managing people included.

One of the differences that makes the difference is best summed up by Michael E. Gerber in his book *The E Myth*.

Gerber's Three Hats of Business

Gerber states that 80 percent of small businesses fail within their first 5 years of business. So his bent in life is to try and determine why this is the case. What is it that the 20 percent do that the 80 percent don't?

He also notes that there is a similar dynamic in large organizations. This is evidenced by 20 percent of departments/divisions leading the organization forward while 80 percent stagnate.

After a closer look Gerber noticed the following:

For any organization, team, division, or department, large or small, to function effectively, there are three roles that need to be addressed:

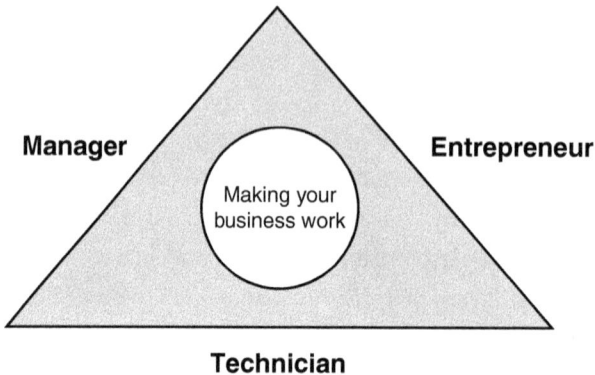

Technician

This is the role of doing the work of the business. It is the role on the production line; the role of dealing with customers; and the role of finding new business. It is the role of doing what it is that the business, team, department, division was set up to do.

Manager

This is the role of managing the work that the business exists to do. Gerber identifies management as having three key components:

- *Budgets:* Most of us think of budgets in purely dollar terms. A clever manager knows that budgets include the management of all resources available to their team. Dollars, people, equipment, time, and perhaps there is a fifth resource emerging—knowledge!
- *Systems:* This is where Gerber makes a major contribution to the field of management. Gerber says that a manager's role is to:

"proceduralise the routine so that we can personalise the exception"

What he is saying here is that if your team has a task they need to perform regularly or routinely, then your role as a manager is to proceduralize it, automate it, put a policy around it, streamline it. Do whatever can be done to make the task as easy as possible so your team members exert the minimal effort to complete the task.

This will leave enough energy, enthusiasm, and brain space for when the exceptions happen. So when a customer complains, when you have the opportunity to make a major bid, when you are asked to do something that is out of the ordinary, you and your team are not only ready but energized.

- *People:* This is the hiring, firing, coaching, counselling, developing, task assignment component of a manager's role. And it is this component that the book is aimed at improving.

The *People* component is your point of leverage for getting your team working so you don't have to. And here is why:

What Gerber discovered often happens is that a small business is born out of a technician (a person with a profession, an architect, an editor, a consultant) who leaves a large business thinking that can do it all by themselves.

So the consummate technician jumps into the marketplace, hangs their shingle over the door, and tries to attract attention to themselves.

Within 5 years, 80 percent of these consummate technicians fail to come to terms with the need for, and the skills required for, the other two roles (i.e., manager and entrepreneur) and will therefore go out of business— usually very dazed and confused!

A similar dynamic happens in large organizations. What many large organizations do is promote the most technically competent person into the role of manager. So the best sales representative gets promoted to the role of sales manager. As a result, not only have we then lost our best revenue producer but we have also put them into a position that requires a totally different set of skills, and we wonder why they struggle!

What is often created is the "Super Technician." A very stressed person who is still wearing the technician's hat and is also being asked to wear the manager's hat. On top of that, their ability to earn a bonus/ overtime is taken away and they are often geographically separated from their team.

The "Super Technician" is an easy beast to spot. They are the ones who are still doing the work. They are often heard talking to their team members saying things like:

What I want you to do is to complete this form and then take it to accounts on level two. They will sign it and keep the pink copy. Then you need to file the yellow copy . . .

If you are having conversations like this with your team members, chances are you are a "Super Technician." You might as well be doing the job yourself.

This is why the hiring, firing, coaching, counselling, developing, and assignment aspects of your role as a manager are an excellent point of leverage. Your aim as a manager is to get them able to do the technical component of your business so you don't have to.

And, yes, there is one other role that we have not discussed yet.

Entrepreneur

In order to clarify what the role of the entrepreneur is all about, let's remind ourselves of how technicians get themselves into trouble by jumping into the marketplace first and then trying to attract attention to themselves.

> Try asking yourself this entrepreneurial-type question . . .
>
> "What is the one thing that's impossible to do in my team, that if I could do it, would completely transform my team output?"

Entrepreneurs do things the other way around. They jump into the marketplace first and do a little research by asking a few questions like:

- What is the market currently up to?
- Where will it be in the next couple of years?
- What pain is the market currently suffering?
- How could that pain be relieved?

Armed with this information, the entrepreneur establishes a product/service, organization, and workplace that meet the need identified.

The technician bases what is possible for them in the future on what they have experienced in the past. The entrepreneur bases what is possible for the market in the future on what has been impossible in the past.

The manager's role in all this? To be able to translate between the two different ways of thinking. To be able to take where the entrepreneur is leading the organization and translate it into a language that helps the technician believe it to be not just possible but probable.

How do you do this? Read on . . .

CHAPTER 2

How to Objectively Analyze the Performance of Your Team

The Issue of Subjectivity

A common criticism of formal performance appraisals is that they are not objective. I have heard many people blame the process, the forms, or the system for being too subjective.

If you think about it, you cannot blame an inanimate object for displaying characteristics that are human. How can a piece of paper be subjective? It's not possible until we include people in the equation. The people who wrote on the paper were subjective but the paper itself cannot be anything but a piece of paper.

So it is people who are not objective when evaluating others' performance. This is because we are both logical and emotional beings and most of the time the two operate in conjunction with each other.

In order to be an exceptional manager, you need to be able to objectively analyze performance. You need to be able to move from fiction to fact, from labels to behaviors.

In the following space, list all of the words that you associate with the ex-tennis player John McEnroe.

The type of words you have recorded will fall into one of two categories: labels or behaviors.

- Labels are value judgments that are based on opinion, are not verifiable and could be debated.
- Behaviors are factual observable or quotable.

For example: In responses to John McEnroe:

Labels	Behaviors
• Bad tempered super brat. • Great tennis player. • He had a sharp wit.	• Received fines for racket abuse. • Was ranked as world's number 1 tennis player four times. • After losing the U.S. Pro Indoor Championships was quoted as saying "This taught me a lesson, but I'm not sure what it is."

In the Workplace

The same dynamic can often happen in the workplace. Managers struggling to give specific performance improving feedback to their team members can find themselves in a sticky situation trying to back up the "labels" they have used to describe performance.

> In order to begin to change peoples' behavior, we need to be able to describe the behavior we don't want repeated and outline the behavior we need.

How to tell if you have used labels to describe performance:

- You have found yourself in a sometimes heated discussion defending your view of their efforts and output during the year.
- You have found yourself going in circles during a performance discussion with a team member.
- You have not seen excellent performance repeated regularly.
- You have not seen poor performance improved.
- Even though you are constantly giving feedback, your team members complain that you never say thanks for a good job done.
- You have found yourself the subject of an unfair dismissal claim.

Being able to identify and express descriptions of behaviors is an issue not just for performance reviews and feedback but also for:
- ○ improving performance of all team members,
- ○ being able to put the right person in the right job,
- ○ unfair dismissal claims.

How to Move from Value Judgments to Behavior Descriptions

Often we find it easier to label or make value judgments using words like:

- lazy
- unreliable
- incompetent
- sloppy
- emotional or
- oxygen thief.

Or even positive labels like:

- good operator
- great to work with
- nice report or
- you're a champion.

It is highly unlikely that being told that you are unreliable, incompetent, or emotional will change your behavior. In most cases it does more damage than good. In order to begin to change people's behavior, we need to be able to *describe the behavior we don't want repeated* and *outline the behavior we need*.

How to Build Behavior Descriptions from Value Judgments . . .

Behaviors are observable and objective. They are what a person does or what a person says. The key to identifying behaviors from value judgments or "labels" is to ask yourself the following question:

What have I seen them do or heard them say that has led me to describe them this way?

Example

Value Judgment	Behavior
"They are a good communicator"	Listens, reflects on others point of view and asks for more information before offering their own contribution.
"They are reliable"	90% of all projects completed within stated timeframes.
"They are lazy"	4 deadlines were missed, 35% of the project time was spent on reworking errors made and late for work 3 times this week.
"They are committed"	They average 9 hours per day and their output is top quality. They often suggest how to improve things. They volunteer to implement improvements.
"They were over emotional"	Started to cry when contradicted. Walked out of the meeting. Raised their voice in discussion with peers.
"Outstanding"	Exceeded sales budgets by 50% consistently. Results are in the top 5% of peer group. Secured 10 new accounts this quarter.
"Disorganized"	Unable to locate files. Fails to meet deadlines. Written material leads to confusion.
"Over Confident"	Consistently interrupts others. Constantly telling others how to do their job. Dominates meetings by talking over the top of others.
"Lacks Initiative"	Carries out minimal duties. Never volunteers to assist others. Fails to attend planned training and development activities.
"Not Committed"	Carries out minimal duties. Consistently late back from lunch. Expresses frustration when receiving requests to complete work. Has refused to do work.

(*continued*)

Value Judgment	Behavior
"Good with Customers"	Always smiles when greeting customers. Listens to the customer and waits until they finish before offering their own suggestions. Follows the organization's standards for telephone techniques.

Use the "Behavior Description Generator" as a step-by-step process to identify behavior descriptions.

To continue with the John McEnroe example:

Behaviour Description Generator

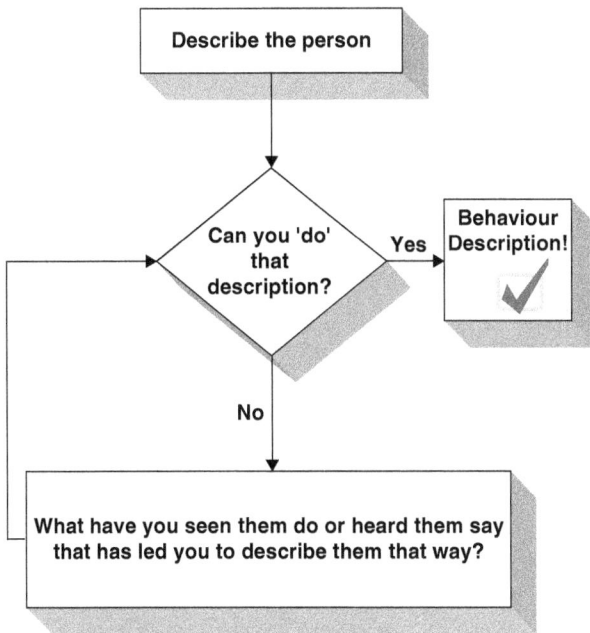

Describe the person
Brat!

Can you "do" that description?

I'm sure you might be thinking, "Yes Rod, I can do Brat. I can do brat very well!" You can't actually "do" brat. It doesn't even make grammatical sense to say it that way.

What you can do is display a series of micro behaviors that when seen together might lead someone to describe you as a brat. It is these micro behaviors that we need to identify. So we need to continue by asking the question:

What have you seen them do or heard them say that has led you to describe them that way?
Smash a tennis racket on the ground.

Can you "Smash a tennis racket on the ground?"—Yes! Then that is a description of behavior

Be rude to the umpire.

Even with this we could ask the question once again: "What have you heard him say that has led you to believe they were being rude?

John said, "I'm surrounded by incompetence. You cannot be serious. The ball was in."

Can you say "I'm surrounded by incompetence. You cannot be serious. The ball was in"?—Yes! Then that is a description of behavior.

So now imagine that you are John McEnroe's manager and you needed him to stop being a brat. Let's say that you had a meeting with him and said, "Listen John, I need you to stop being a brat."

Chances are you would either end up in a debate about the word brat with John asking you for specific examples of when and where or you would get into an argument that would lead to one of you walking out on the other.

Now imagine that you sat John down and said: "John, from here on there will be no more smashing your tennis racket on the ground, there will be no more smashing drink stands with tennis rackets, and there will be no more saying 'I'm surrounded by incompetence. You cannot be serious. The ball was in.'"

Now with people like John McEnroe there are, of course, no guarantees. What we can say is that we have dramatically reduced the chance of debate or argument as we have made the feedback undeniable.

In fact imagine how powerful the feedback would be if we then followed this up with an equally specific examples of behaviors that we would like John to replace his current behaviors with.

From now on John, when you disagree with a call I need you to stay quiet, turn around and start preparing for the next point. You may even say to the linesman, 'That would have been a tough one to call. Well done.'

Value Judgment to Behavior Descriptions

Skills Practice

Now practice the process with a few labels you might use to describe your team members. Think of some of your team members and identify the value judgments you would use to describe their performance and record these in the "Value Judgments" column. Then ask yourself:

What have I seen them do or heard them say that has led me to describe them this way?

and record your responses in the "Behavior" column.

NB: As a rule of thumb, if you are unable to come up with at least three specific behaviors for that label, chances are that the label is inaccurate and you will have just discovered some of your own subjectivity.

Value Judgment	Behavior

Ability, Attitude, and Resources

There are three main components that effectuate a person's ability to perform. They are as follows.

Ability

An individual's ability to do something is dependent on things like:

- Skill level
- Experience
- Knowledge.

Obviously, a person who has a greater degree of ability is better positioned to deliver better results.

Attitude

An individual's attitude to do something is dependent on things like:

- Enthusiasm
- Commitment
- Values/Ethics.

I'm sure you can think of people you work with who have a "good attitude" and those who have a "bad attitude." We intuitively recognize the effect that this has on the quality of work completed.

Resources

As mentioned earlier, resources are typically things such as:

- Money
- Support from other people
- Materials and equipment
- Time
- Knowledge—the recording and retrieval of what individuals in an organization learn.

There are other organizational resources that can also affect performance:

- Strategy and business plan
- Leadership styles
- Work practices, procedures, and policies
- Systems
- Structure of the business.

As a manager, the manipulation of resources is a book in itself and, in some respects, resources exist outside of the individual whose performance we are trying to improve. Often people will use a "resource"-type issue to justify poor performance:

"Well if only we had a bigger budget we could do that!"
"That's all very well but our people are already stretched to the maximum."
"I'll tell you what! You provide me with an updated lap top and a company car and I'll be able to do what you want."
"I don't have the time. That deadline is unrealistic."

Sound familiar?

That is not to say that these comments aren't valid some of the time. There are of course stressed people out there who do need certain materials and equipment and a realistic deadline to do what it is we are asking them to do.

What we need to do as a manager is to sort the wheat from the chaff and recognize that often this is the technician arguing for what they believe to be possible based on the past. And remember that part of our role as a manager is to help technicians discover how to create the future, not recreate the past.

In order to do this our starting point is their ability, their attitude, and what we know about labels and behaviors.

Steps to an Objective Analysis of Your Team Members' Ability and Attitude

Before you write on the following page, photocopy it, or scan it into your computer. You may need it more than once.

Record your team members' names down the left-hand side of the page.

1. Record the main responsibilities of their position in the next column.
2. Ask yourself what have you seen them do or heard them say that would indicate a high or low level of ability? Record your answers in the next column.
3. Ask yourself what have you seen them do or heard them say that would indicate a high or low level of attitude? Record your answers in the next column.
4. Rate out of 10 their ability and their attitude based on the behaviors you have identified.
5. Leave the "Leadership Tactic" column blank for now.

For example:

Team member	Tasks/ duties	Ability behaviors	Attitude behaviors	Leadership tactic
Liam Collins	Sales	110% of budget for the last three quarters 10/10	Volunteers to take on a larger territory 10/10	
	Weekly reports	100% accurate 10/10	Reports have been late for the last 5 weeks 2/10	
	Product knowledge	Achieved a score of 70% in Product Knowledge test. Pass mark is 85% 4/10	Often asks for coaching and extra reading on product range 7/10	

Diagnosing My Team Members' Leadership Needs

Team member	Tasks/duties	Ability behaviors	Attitude behaviors	Leadership tactic

What Would Happen If I Didn't Bother?

Without objective performance analysis as a foundation for your performance improvement tactics, you run the unnecessary risk of:

- wasting your time
- wasting your team members time
- making the working relationship worse than it needs to be
- being labeled a poor manager/leader.

CHAPTER 3

Tactics to Improve Performance

How to Increase Your Leadership Flexibility

Have you ever been to a management or leadership training program where they spent time analyzing your leadership style?

You know the ones. You fill out a questionnaire, your responses are tallied and the score gives you an indication about your leadership preference, how you prefer to respond when in a leadership context.

These are a great place to start understanding how you interact with your team members and other people in general. They are also great fun to "find out about yourself" since self-awareness is an excellent first step to improvement.

There is, however, a word of warning with this approach. If the analysis instrument is of low quality, if the session is run poorly or superficially, it can do more harm than good.

Many a time I have seen people leave a poorly run leadership style session wearing their style as a badge and using it as an excuse for inflexible, inappropriate, and ill-informed behaviors.

Twenty years of research into what makes leaders successful in an organization and what derails them has been conducted by the Centre for Creative Leadership based in the USA. Their results show that the most consistent response to the question "What makes a great leader?" is *flexibility*! (Slightly ironic that we are so inflexible about the need for flexibility!)

Merely learning what leadership style *you* are does not build flexibility. As illustrated in the preceding paragraphs, it can actually lead to very much the opposite.

The best way to build leadership flexibility is to *analyze your team member's performance* and *then* determine what style of leadership would have the greatest impact on improving their performance.

This approach is:

- Team member focused and therefore less self-centered. It requires you to focus on the people you manage first and then your own behaviors.
- Far more effective. It produces better results because they are tailored to the needs of the team member.
- Builds flexibility. It enables you to expand your leadership style to encompass a variety of different styles.

If, as a leader or manager, you only have one way of interacting with your team members, then every situation will appear as if that response is appropriate.

We have started to do this by analyzing performance in terms of ability and attitude. We now have a good distinction on what creates poor, good, and great performance.

> If the only tool you have in your tool box in a hammer . . . then everything is going to look like a nail.

Now we need to use this information about our team members to determine what "style of leadership" would bring the best out of our team. And the answer is quite simply different strokes for different folks.

This is not to be illusive. It is because the formula for an exceptional leader is dependent on many variables. Here are just a few:

- different team members
- different tasks
- different times.

What we need is a model that will start us thinking about these variables and at least provide us with somewhere to begin. Otherwise analysis becomes paralysis and we end up doing nothing.

So let's take the two components of performance that we started with and build a model.

The Leadership Tactic Grid

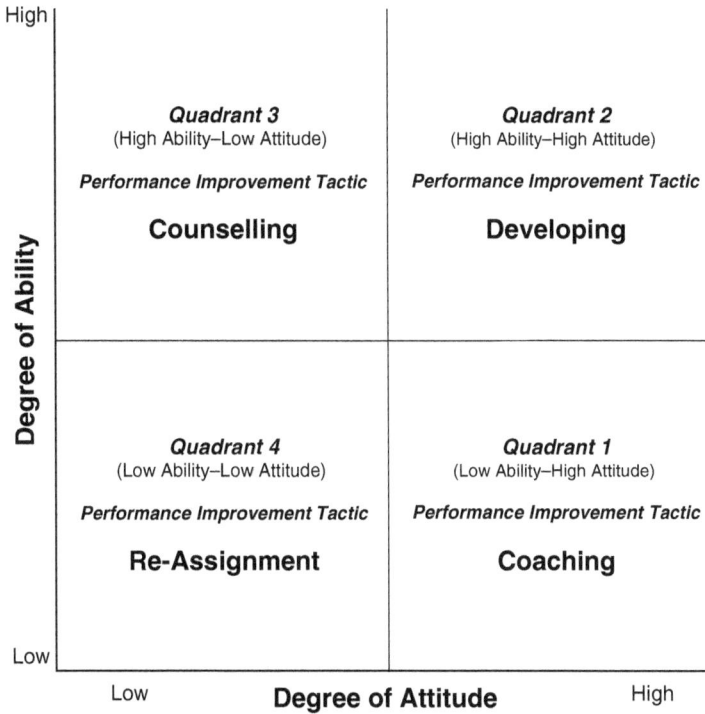

High

Degree of Ability

Quadrant 3
(High Ability–Low Attitude)

Performance Improvement Tactic

Counselling

Quadrant 2
(High Ability–High Attitude)

Performance Improvement Tactic

Developing

Quadrant 4
(Low Ability–Low Attitude)

Performance Improvement Tactic

Re-Assignment

Quadrant 1
(Low Ability–High Attitude)

Performance Improvement Tactic

Coaching

Low

Low   **Degree of Attitude**   High

Source: P. Zigarmi, D. Zigarmi, and K.H. Blanchard. 1999. *'Situational Leadership Grid'*—
Leadership and the One Minute Manager: Increasing Effectiveness through Situational Leadership. New
York: William Morrow & Co. ISBN: 0688039693.

The key with this model is to remember that it is contextual. This means that the one person could be performing in all the different quadrants depending on the task that they are doing, the day that they believe they are having, the people they need to work with etc.

As we outline each of the following quadrants, you might start to think about particular contexts and particular team members that you manage.

Quadrant 1: *Low Ability–high Attitude*

This is where people want to do a good job, are enthusiastic, and have had no previous experience. They will display high commitment and low competence.

Some examples include:

- someone who has just been promoted into a new job
- a new team member
- the duties in the job have changed
- new technology or processes have been introduced.

A good leader would aim here to improve the level of competence by being a coach.

Quadrant 2: *High Ability–high Attitude*

This is where people are able to do the task at hand and they enjoy doing it. This is obviously the ideal! A major component of the leader's role is to ensure that as many of their team as possible fall into this quadrant for as many duties as possible.

A good leader would aim to recognize, reward and stretch a highly committed and highly competent performer through development.

Quadrant 3: *High Ability–low Attitude*

This is where people know how to do the job and do not enjoy doing it or do not want to do it. There are many reasons why a person's commitment is not with the task at hand. These include:

- they are bored with that particular task
- the task is considered menial
- the task is considered too time consuming or too complex
- the person's commitment is currently elsewhere (personal, social, or family issues).

A good leader would address the cause of the low commitment through counselling.

Quadrant 4: *Low Ability–low Attitude*

This is where people don't know how to do the task and don't want to learn. A good leader here would reassign.

Now, often when people first see the word "Reassign" used in this context, they often think something like our little friend here . . .

It is easy to jump to the conclusion that we should sack this person and hire someone else to do the job.

This is an expensive decision. It would cost an organization far more in both dollar costs and intangible costs to terminate an employment and find a new employee than it often does working with the person to determine what alternatives are available.

Remember, it could be that the team member is fantastic at other more important parts of their job than just this one area that they don't know how to do and don't want to learn.

Alternatives to sacking include:

- give the task to someone else
- determine if the task can be done by computer or other machinery
- have an external organization do the work
- hire a contractor or consultant
- ask "What would happen if this task was not done? Would it really matter?"

A good manager will be able to use a situation like this to find new and creative ways of improving their team's output through reassignment. Referring back to the analysis we made earlier of your team members' ability and attitude levels, we can now assess which tactic would be best to improve their performance in the tasks you identified.

Team member	Tasks/ duties	Ability behaviors	Attitude behaviors	Leadership tactic
Liam Collins	Sales	110% of budget for the last three quarters 10/10	Volunteers to take on a larger territory 10/10	Develop
	Weekly reports	100% accurate 10/10	Reports have been late for the last 5 weeks 2/10	Counsel
	Product knowledge	Achieved a score of 70% in Product Knowledge test. Pass mark is 85% 4/10	Often asks for coaching and extra reading on product range 7/10	Coach

CHAPTER 4

Coaching

Are You Insane?

Have you ever explained something to a team member a dozen times only to find that they stuffed it up again?

If so then stop telling and start coaching.

> The definition of insanity is doing the same thing over and over again and expecting different results!
>
> —*Albert Einstein*

By that definition we are all insane to some extent. I got home from work the other day and was feeling a little hungry. So I looked in the fridge but there was nothing there except this half-dead over-cultured tomato. So I closed the fridge door and looked in the pantry. No, nothing there that would be quick enough, appetizing enough, healthy enough. So what did I do? Look back in the fridge. Maybe something has cooked itself while I was looking in the pantry!!?!?!?

> **If you have told someone something more than once and they still don't get it then stop telling and start coaching!**

Just Send Them on a Training Course. That'll Fix 'em!

Let's make two things perfectly clear.

1. Training and coaching are two different things. Training is something I do. Coaching is something you should be doing.
2. Unless the training is of exceptional quality, training courses rarely change anything.

A poor manager will send their team members on a training course and then do nothing else to improve competence.

A great manager develops a coaching program that might include a training component. For example, a coaching program to improve Liam Collins product knowledge could include the following steps:

1. Meet with Liam and review results of Product Knowledge test to identify areas of need.
2. Design coaching session to provide Liam with missing knowledge.
3. Liam to attend the organization's Product Knowledge training program.
4. Meet with Liam after the training to debrief the training course.
5. Liam to re-sit Product Knowledge test.
6. Ask Liam to manage a client, which will test his newly acquired product knowledge.
7. Meet with Liam to see how he is going with the client.

If you were Liam, It would be near-impossible not to become a product knowledge expert after that level of attention.

What we will be looking at in this part of the book is tips, tools, and techniques on how to hold a coaching conversation.

Using Three Logical Levels to Get Your Message Across

Try the following exercise.

In the space provided following these few paragraphs, try to draw a picture based on my written description. As you do this, notice what you are thinking and what you are feeling as you try to follow the instructions.

I want you to draw an hourglass shape with a rounded top and bottom. Now on the bottom of the hourglass I want you to draw two tall thin rectangles that start about one-third of the way down the bottom half of the hourglass and extend a tiny bit beyond the bottom of the hourglass shape. Now draw two parallel squiggly lines starting at the bottom right-hand point of the hourglass and extending out to the right. Now draw a circle about the same size as the top part of the hourglass. Draw this circle on top of the top part of the hourglass. Now put two small triangles on the outside of the circle, two small circles inside the circle, another small triangle inside the circle, and a line.

How'd you go?

Not easy, is it? Frustrating isn't it? Want to ask questions to get it accurate, don't you?

This is how a poor, even an average, manager would go about coaching.

- I tell you
- You listen and then go and do
- Don't ask any questions because much of what I say is via e-mail, manual, or memo
- I'll ask you "Do you understand?" and your triggered response will be "Yes!"

An exceptional coach understands, either consciously or intuitively, that instructions are best communicated on three logical levels.

1. Concept
2. Principles
3. Details

Let's try the same activity again. This time we will use the three logical levels as a guide to construct the message.

1. **Concept**
   I'd like you to draw a cat much like a child might draw a cat.
2. **Principles**
   a. Before we start I'd like to establish some ground rules around how we are going to do this.

    i. Ground rule 1. Please read each instruction before putting your pen to paper

    ii. Ground rule 2. If you are unsure then reread the instruction or refer to the principles or concept.

    iii. Ground rule 3. Feel free once we have finished to add your own touches to make the cat as recognizable as possible.

  b. There are three key components to drawing a cat:

    i. Drawing the body

    ii. Drawing the legs and tail

    iii. Drawing the head and face

  We will draw each component one at a time.

3. **Details**

In the space provided following these paragraphs, please draw the cat using these instructions:

  i. Drawing the body.

  I want you to draw an hourglass shape with a rounded top and bottom.

  ii. Drawing the legs and tail.

  First the legs. On the bottom of the hourglass I want you to draw two tall thin rectangles that start about one-third of the way down the bottom half of the hourglass and extend a tiny bit beyond the bottom of the hourglass shape.

  Now the tail. Draw two parallel squiggly lines starting at the bottom right-hand point of the hourglass and extending out to the right.

iii. Drawing the head and face.

First the head. Draw a circle about the same size as the top part of the hourglass. Draw this circle on top of the top part of the hourglass.

And the face. Draw the ears by putting two small triangles on the outside of the circle. The eyes are two small circles inside the large circle (or head). The nose is another small triangle inside the circle and the mouth is drawn by a single line.

Compare your result with what I had in mind.

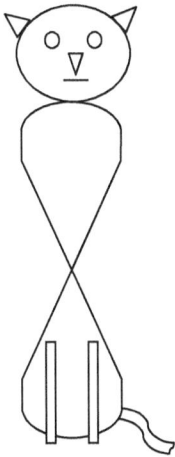

Yes, it takes longer to coach someone than tell them, but compare the time coaching takes with the time, cost of errors, and level of frustration of telling them a dozen times and they still don't get it!

How to Format Your Coaching Session

Let's say that it was Christmas morning. You wake up, you rush to the Christmas tree, you rip open your pressies and let's say for the sake of argument that you received a new computer. Let's also say that you have never set up a computer from scratch before.

Different people learn in different ways. For example:

- Some people will look for the manual. If a job's worth doing, do it once, do it right!
- Some people would just start plugging things in and seeing what happens.
- Some people might phone up a friend of theirs who is an expert at setting up computers and watch what they do.
- Some people do several of the above in a specific order. For example, I would start by plugging things and seeing what happens. Then after a while I would get stuck. Then the words of my dear Dad would haunt me . . . "If all else fails, read the instructions." So out comes the manual. I pore over that for a while, get a little further and then call that good friend of mine who can set up computers and watch them sort out the mess I've made.

Learning styles have been studied by many people. David Kolb, Kathy Kolbe and Bernice McCarthy have made some outstanding contributions to this area of knowledge.

David A. Kolb's model of experiential learning can be found in many discussions of the theory and practice of adult education, informal education, and lifelong learning.

For over 25 years, Kathy Kolbe has been dedicated to helping people improve their lives by showing them better ways to use their talents. Her first mission was to improve the educational opportunities of elementary and high school-aged children through developing a learning styles questionnaire that will identify what is your preferred learning style. Worth doing if you have the time. Check out www.kolbe.com

If, however, you are after something a little more practical from a manager's perspective, then a summary of the work done be Bernice McCarthy would be ideal. You only have to type the name "Bernice McCarthy" into a search engine on the internet to gauge the scale and practicality of her work.

Bernice McCarthy realized that most people are capable of learning through all of those methods. She also realized that when coaching, few people have the time or skill to identify the learning preference of the person we are trying to coach and then design something specifically for them.

Instead she noticed that each learner is asking specific questions in a specific order and that if we answer all of those questions in that specific order, we will maximize the likelihood that the trainee increases knowledge, skill, and attitude.

Notice the Difference Between the Following

Following are two messages. Both share the same aim. As you read the two messages, imagine they are addressed to you personally and notice your response. What are you thinking or feeling directly after reading each message.

Message 1

Congratulations! You have been selected to attend a "Performance Management Program" that will be running in the conference room on the 10th, 11th, and 12th of next month starting at 8.30 a.m.

In an ongoing effort to improve the skills of our managers, senior management and HR have developed these programs and you will be required to design a Personal Development plan in conjunction with the course.

Message 2

Now contrast that with this message. Imagine that your manager has sat you down and said the following:

> I was remembering our conversation the other day and I was thinking that you are right. It can be very difficult trying to manage team members sometimes. Trying to manage people who seem to have a different agenda to yours, trying to get things done right first time so you don't end up having to fix everyone else's mistakes and trying to make the most out of being the meat in the sandwich between your team members and senior management. It's not easy.

> So I was thinking that there must be a way of reducing that stress and frustration, increasing the likelihood that team members do things right first time and also a way of making sure that you are able to state your case in the most persuasive manner possible to senior management.

> Then I came across this 'Performance Management Program' that will be running in the conference room on the 10th, 11th, and 12th of next month starting at 8.30 a.m. I figured that if we drew up a Personal Development plan that addresses the things that are making it difficult for you at the moment we might be able to make your job a little less stressful.

> "What do you think?"

The First Question You Have to Answer . . . "Why"

It's pretty hard to not prefer the second message. Why is that? The aim of the message is the same, the main thing that has changed is that in the first message we have told you "*what*" first and then we have justified it with a "*why.*"

Message 1

What

Congratulations! You have been selected to attend a "Performance Management Program" that will be running in the conference room on the 10th, 11th, and 12th of next month starting at 8.30 a.m.

Why

In an ongoing effort to improve the skills of our managers, senior management and HR have developed these programs and you will be required to design a Personal Development plan in conjunction with the course.

Message 2

Why

I was remembering our conversation the other day and I was thinking that you are right. It can be very difficult trying to manage team members sometimes. Trying to manage people who seem to have a different agenda from yours, trying to get things done right first time so you don't end up having to fix everyone else's mistakes and trying to make the most out of being the meat in the sandwich between your team members and senior management. It's not easy.

What

"Then I came across this "Performance Management Program" that will be running in the conference room on the 10th, 11th, and 12th of next month starting at 8.30 a.m.

So I was thinking that there must be a way of reducing that stress and frustration, increasing the likelihood that team members do things right first time and also a way of making sure that you are able to state your case in the most persuasive manner possible to senior management.

I figured that if we drew up a Personal Development plan that addresses the things that are making it difficult for you at the moment, we might be able to make your job a little less stressful.

"What do you think?"

In an effort to increase our communications efficiency, we sometimes trade its effectiveness.

In the second message not only have we reversed the order to "*why*" first and then "*what*," we have also repositioned the reason "why" from an organization level to a personal level. We have included several what's in it for me (WIIFMs).

We will talk more about how to supercharge your WIIFMs later. For the moment let's continue with formatting your coaching session.

Think of all the methods and times we want to get a message across that would benefit from having the audience interested before we open the kimono completely. In the corporate world these methods include:

- Meeting
- Memo
- Manual
- Mail
- Message

Take the opportunity below to think about all the times you would like to increase your audience's level of "buy-in" to your message (home, work, socially . . .).

Now That You Have Their Attention . . . "What"

Now that you have their attention, they will be more receptive to "*What*" you have to say.

In order to maximize the likelihood that your message is understood, try presenting your message using the logical levels that we identified earlier:

1. Concept
2. Principles
3. Details

That's All Very Well, but . . . "How"

As mentioned at the beginning of this book . . . there is an old Chinese saying:

I hear and I forget,
I see and I remember,
I do and I understand!

It is highly unlikely that you would become an excellent swimmer by attending a lecture and then watching someone else swim. At some stage you're going to have to get wet!

A good coach will use all the above methods to ensure that their trainee has the best chance that they are going to be able to keep themselves afloat.

The *hear* part happens as we answer the question *what*. The *see* and *do* comes under the *how* component.

This requires you as a coach to demonstrate the skill, competency, and process, and then allow the trainee to practice.

Yeah, but Let's Just Say . . . "What else/what if"

Once we start to feel a degree of comfort with new learning, we gain a deeper understanding by testing possibilities, changing context, and toying with content. This is often punctuated with questions that include words like "*What else*" and "*What if.*"

- "What would happen if . . ."
- "What else is there to know about . . ."
- "Let's just say for the sake of argument that . . ."
- "What will we need to do if . . ."
- "What else can we say about . . ."

Once again, a good coach will not only be prepared for these questions, but they will also ask a few themselves to prompt the deeper understanding.

Many of the "*What else/what if*" questions are answered during the process, particularly during the doing or "*how*" frame. Therefore, these questions are best asked and answered after the trainee has had an initial experience with the learning. That is, after the *Why, what,* and *how.*

How to Supercharge Your "Why" Frame

Have you ever wanted to reduce the level of negativity that you believe a trainee or team member might have toward a message that you have to deliver?

Have you ever wanted to reduce the number of times you find yourself debating the merits of a policy or procedure and having to take the "management line?"

Have you ever wanted to increase the level of buy-in a team member or other manager has for your idea or message?

Have you ever had a new team member take over a job and you wanted to maintain the high level of quality that has been established in the past?

Then you will love knowing how to supercharge your "why" frames.

There are three words that marketers, advertisers, and entrepreneurs have known about and used for years. They are very powerful words in the right context. All products and services that exist in the marketplace today do so because the potential users/buyers can see how it will do one, two, or all three of these words for them.

Next time you see an advertisement on TV, in the papers, in magazines, on the internet, on the radio, or particularly a billboard (a good billboard ad will convey its message within seconds), notice which one, two, or all three of these words are either used explicitly or implied.

- **Reduce**
  People will part with large sums of money, time, and effort if they can see how doing so will reduce their:
  - Pain
  - Annoyance
  - Frustration
  - Effort
  - Stress
  - Errors
  - Wastage
  - Time spent doing stuff they don't want to do.
- **Improve/increase**
  People will part with large sums of money, time, and effort if they can see how doing so will improve or increase their:
  - Pleasure
  - Leisure

- ○ Enjoyment
- ○ Ease
- ○ Results
- ○ Happiness
- ○ Accuracy
- ○ Time spent doing stuff they love doing.
- **Maintain**
  People will part with large sums of money, time, and effort if they can see how doing so will maintain their:
  - ○ Security
  - ○ Predictability
  - ○ Safety
  - ○ Tradition
  - ○ Lifestyle
  - ○ Expectations.

Think about how this is true for you on four levels.

1. Your organization's products and services
2. Your team's products or services
3. Your team members' roles
4. Your role as a manager.

So now you can supercharge your "*why*" frame with statements like:

I was remembering our conversation the other day and I was thinking that you are right. It can be very difficult trying to manage team members sometimes. Trying to manage people who seem to have a different agenda to yours, trying to get things done right first time so you don't end up having to fix everyone else's mistakes and trying to make the most out of being the meat in the sandwich between your team members and senior management. It's not easy.

So I was thinking that there must be a way of **reducing** that stress and frustration, **increasing** the likelihood that team members do things right first time and also a way of making sure that you are able to state your case in the most persuasive manner possible to senior management while **maintaining** job security.

Please keep in mind that coaching works best when the ability is low and the attitude is high. If you have analyzed your team members' performance correctly, there should be less need to "supercharge" your "why" frame as the trainee should already be enthusiastic and eager.

That does not mean that you can ignore it altogether. Even enthusiastic people need relevance.

Pre-framing the Practice

Have you ever been in school, university, training programs, or other teacher–student scenario and the teacher has said something like . . . "Ok. This will be in the exam." Instantly a previously uninterested group of students pick up pens, arrange papers, and become alert.

Imagine how much better you would have done in examinations if all your teachers had done the same thing. The fact is, of course, that many teachers do not. The result is that the student does not know what to look for in the mountains of information that is presented to them and is therefore more likely to switch off and miss the most important bits.

The same thing can happen with a poor coach. A poor coach will ask their trainee to do something but not provide the trainee with anything to "look for" in the activity. So the opportunity to allow discovery, the opportunity to increase depth and width of learning has been lost.

Pre-framing is a way of giving people's thoughts direction before they try or experience something. The aim is to increase the likelihood that the trainee finds what it is you need them to find in the activity and are then more able to discuss it with some degree of insight afterwards.

The key to doing this well is to send the trainees' thoughts in the right direction without giving them the answer. An example follows.

Giving the Answer	Pre-framing
As you are talking to this client, you will have to wait until you have built rapport before you can offer solutions	As you are talking to this client, I'd like you to notice how you know when you have built enough rapport to start offering potential solutions
As you try this new procedure, I'd like you to notice how much quicker, easier, and more accurate it is.	As you try this new procedure, I'd like you to notice what you notice about time, ease, and accuracy.
As you are managing this project, I'd like you to use the cost control measures we have in place. I'd also like you to increase quality and make sure you meet your deadlines.	As you are managing this project, I'd like you to identify the three key things that would reduce costs, improve quality, and maintain deadlines.
As you do this, notice how much better you would feel.	As you do this, I'd like you to notice what you are thinking and what you are feeling and we will talk about that afterwards.

Think about all the opportunities you have had throughout your day to coach your team members. Sometimes coaching happens on the fly in corridors, over lunch, in tea rooms, in a meeting, after work at the pub.

Pre-framing is an excellent way of making every conversation a coaching conversation.

How to Provide Balanced Feedback That Improves Performance

Have you ever noticed how some people have a preference to see the glass as half empty and others have a preference to see the glass as half full? Neither is better, it depends on the context as to which is going to be most useful.

When on holidays, you will probably enjoy yourself a lot more if you are noticing what is good about where you are, if you are noticing what you can do, if you are noticing who the nice people are.

When you are working on something that requires a high level of safety, it is probably better to notice what is missing, what is inaccurate, and what is not up to the standard.

A poor manager will only notice what it is their preference to notice.

So, for example, if I had just completed a piece of paperwork and brought it to you for checking and your preference was for seeing the glass as half empty, your response might be something like . . . "Ok. You've forgot to complete Section 3 . . . That's not the right code . . . and you haven't got finance to sign it yet."

If your preference was to see the glass as half full, you might respond by saying . . . "Wow! This is great work. I love how you remembered to complete section two . . . your handwriting is really neat, so it's easy to read . . . And you remembered to stamp it. Lots of people forget that bit." Then as I walk away you fix all the errors yourself.

When you are a coach, it is best to notice both.

There is a useful method that will help you do this. Use the "EDI" (affectionately known as "Eddy") system to help keep your feedback constructive, supportive, and balanced.

Effective

- What did the person do that was really effective? Please be as specific as possible—people love to know exactly what they did well!

Do more of

- What did the person do, that if they did it even more or even bigger or just more often, would really make an impact? Again be specific.

Improve

- What would be your *positive* suggestions for improvement? How could they do it even better next time? State your suggestions positively, i.e., what they should *be* doing, not what they should *stop* doing.

Finally end up with some overall, global statements of appreciation, linking back to what they did well. Here you don't need to be specific, so feel free to be global and fluffy!

An Example Coaching Session

Coaching Tool	Example Conversation
"Why" frame	Liam! Thanks for coming in. Let's take a seat. I was thinking the other day how overwhelming it can be in your first few months in a new position, particularly when there is so much to learn about things like the territory management system, using the laptop, and the sales software we have and also acquiring the product knowledge. All the different customized options that we have for different clients can be truly paralyzing. I was also thinking that there must be some way of making the first few months as easy as possible, some way of reducing the sense of being overwhelmed and something that we could do to maintain and increase you profile within the team. So what I'd like to do is discuss with you some of the areas where you and I believe we could create the greatest leverage with your results by spending some time working together. How does that sound?
"What" frame	Alright. One of the areas I think will provide us with a great point of leverage would be product knowledge. How are you going with product knowledge at the moment? What I thought we could talk about today is how to like customer needs with the customizable options of our products.
Concept	The concept here is to build a product around what our customer needs rather than simply offering an "off-the-shelf" solution.
Principles	The key principles around doing this are to identify what the customer's priorities are when it comes to speed, quality, and cost.
Details	The details here are: Let's say, for example, that a client mentions that they have a tight deadline. Then we would talk about product A because it is our fastest option. If the customer mentioned that they are sick of breakdowns, we can talk about product B as it is our highest quality product. If the customer talks of having a tight budget, we can talk about product C as it is our cheapest option.
"How" frame	So let's test these ideas. Let's say we had a client who was in the supermarket industry and I'll be the client and you be the representative and I'll drop a few hints about what I'm looking for and we will see how we go.

Pre-framing	Now before we start. On the one hand, this is just a silly role play that is different from reality and all about acting. On one hand that's correct. On the other hand, as we do this, what I want you to notice is what are some of the trigger words and phrases that led you to select a certain product over the others and we will talk about that afterwards. Ok. So here we go . . . (Role play a client situation)
Effectively	Well done. What I think you did effectively there was to identify my needs. You recognized that I was after a product that was going to fit into an already tight process time wise.
Do more of	Something you might want to do more of is asking questions. You started with a few at the beginning and I loved it because I got to play expert. If you could continue asking questions up to the point where you recommend the product, that would be great.
Improve	And in order to put the icing on the cake, something you might want to look at is building rapport before offering solutions. I think that there was a lot of effort going into identifying product that there was no attempt at building rapport between us.
"What else/what if" frame	So what were some of the trigger words and phrases that you identified? What type of clients do we currently have or are we targeting that would fit that mold? What could we do if a client asked for all three, speed, quality, and cost? What would happen if you didn't match product to need?

CHAPTER 5

Developing

Why Develop?

In the space below list the reasons why you left previous jobs. Be honest now . . . no one is watching.

Common reasons include:

- Bored
- Gone as far as I could go
- Done as much as I could do
- Manager was a dropkick
- Better offer
- Chance to develop myself further

Most of these reasons are linked to the fact that few managers (only the really good ones) recognize top talent and work to keep them as much as possible by developing them. If you have some people in your team that you would like to keep for a while then I would strongly recommend that you develop them.

Some arguments that are often voiced at this stage are:

- "Why would we want to spend our organization's resources developing people when chances are that they will leave and take their skills to our competitors?"

  In some cases you are right. There are organizations that are known out there as great training grounds for certain industries. A great place to cut your teeth and then move on.

  The thing to remember is that most people will change jobs, organizations, even careers, from time to time. What we have while they are with us is an opportunity to make the relationship as mutually beneficial as possible.

  The law of reciprocity states—what you give is what you get. If as a manager you give nothing, then . . .

- "Sometimes it's just best that they move on. Some people have just grown stale and are becoming bitter, so we don't want to keep them."

  Couldn't agree more with this one. There are indeed times that it would be better to end the working relationship and cut some people loose.

  Once again, let us remember when it is appropriate to develop. Development works best with people who have a high level of ability and a high level of attitude. If someone is not committed to their work or their organization or their team . . . then I would say that is a low attitude and then we would be counseling, not developing.

If you accept the 80/20 rule, you will agree that often a poor manager will spend 80 percent of their time dealing with the 20 percent of team members who are causing them problems while spending only 20 percent of their time working with the 80 percent of the team that is doing OK to great!

Development is a way of evening up that imbalance.

Three Key Principles to Development

There are three key principles to keep in mind when we use the word develop, and they are:

1. Recognize
2. Reward
3. Stretch

1. **Recognize**

   If you have a person who is displaying high ability and high attitude then you need to recognize those behaviors by providing feedback. In doing so you are also increasing the likelihood that those behaviors are repeated.

2. **Reward**

   Anyone who has worked in a place without incentive will know how de-motivating it can be. People have more reason to read books at work, do the crossword, gossip etc. when there is no incentive or reward to go beyond what is expected of them.

   I can remember working for an organization that gave me a Christmas bonus. The bonus was an all-expenses-paid trip to Norfolk Island for my wife and me. It was a perfect gift for us as we love walking, sightseeing, relaxing, and history.

   If the organization gave us the same amount of money in a cash bonus, it would have gone to the mortgage and I would have barely noticed the reward. As it was in the form of a wonderful trip, I will never forget the organization and what's more the manager who arranged the bonus remains one of the few managers I would class as exceptional!

   For your reward to really hit the mark, you will need to know what turns your team member on. What do they like and dislike? Where are they headed?

3. **Stretch**

   No matter how complex your job and no matter how simple you would like your job to be, the fact remains, doing the same thing over and over again, day in and day out, week in and week out, eventually becomes mind-numbingly boring.

It is true that different people like a different amount of stretch. It is also true that most people want a degree of stretch. It is often called "variety" or "change" or "something new." No matter how it is spelt, people like to be stretched.

An exceptional manager will identify how much stretch and in what direction.

As with coaching, an exceptional manager will also recognize that development does not mean sending them to a training course.

A Development Process

A simple process to follow would be:

1. Start with recognition
2. Identify their needs and wants
3. Identify development tactics
4. Build the development plan
5. Implement the development plan
6. Monitor progress

Let's look at each of these in more detail.

Start with Recognition

The first step in developing someone is to let them know why you are developing them. Provide them with some feedback. This feedback needs to be:

1. Specific
2. Positive
3. Genuine

Now I have a theory. If providing positive, genuine, and specific feedback was an Olympic sport, Australia would come a sad last. By and large we are pathetic at providing positive, genuine, specific feedback. In fact we tend to do the exact opposite!

Hey jerk! This guy is a complete loser. How are you, you old bugger.

. . . and somehow that means we like each other. I remember working for an organization in the telecommunications industry that held senior positions open for expatriate Americans. After they were told they got the job and before they left to come to Australia, they would attend a cultural awareness program. In this they were brought up to speed on how to work with Australians.

Some of the more interesting points were:

- Good service in Australia means having the following conversation
  "Can I help you?"
  "No thanks just looking."
  "OK then I leave you alone then"
- "She'll be right mate" means I know that it looks as though I'm doing nothing and I can understand your sense of urgency but with a couple of mates and a case of beer we'll knock it over in an afternoon.
- Jack is as good as his master. Just because you have a bigger title than mine does not mean that you are better off to make a more accurate decision than me. I've been around too and you tall poppies need to come down a couple of notches.

And of course . . .

- Personal abuse is a sign of affection and respect.

The point is that if you wish to be seen as an exceptional manager, you are going to have to get used to doing some things that might go against the grain. Providing genuine, positive, and specific feedback could be one of them.

We have already covered a tool that will help us here and that is the behavior description generator. This will ensure that your feedback is specific and will increase the likelihood that the development opportunity is linked to some specific behaviors that you would like to see repeated.

Notice the difference between the following:

> Nice work Anna. That's great. It's just what we needed. Thanks so much. Having you around is great. I think that is the second or third time you've done something like this. Thanks again.

Now compare with:

> Nice work Anna. That's great. We needed a report that used a different methodology to the one we have always used in the past and your inclusion of the analysis really gives it an edge we didn't have. I also love how you have identified three possible courses of action, clearly outlined the advantages and disadvantages of each and then recommended option 3. This is the third time you have improved our processes around here. Thanks again Anna!

With the first one there is no specificity. So it becomes difficult for Anna to repeat her good work. On top of this, while we are providing her with positive feedback it will not create nearly the impact the second example would provide.

Identify Their Needs and Wants

Remember that we are dealing with someone here who is both competent and committed. Someone who has probably made your job a lot easier over the past few months. This is an opportunity to give something back. To reward, recognize, and stretch in proportion with their efforts above and beyond the call of duty.

This can be one of the most enjoyable and fulfilling parts of a manager's role if you can tailor the development to suit the specific individual that you are trying to develop. One size does not fit all and a "sheep dip" approach to development of your peak performers can do more damage than good.

So the skill becomes how to tailor the development to meet the needs and wants of the individual.

Have you ever been to an interview where you were asked that question that sends some into a complete tailspin and others into some endless diatribe . . .

So, where do you see yourself in 5 years' time?

It can be a bit of a non-question when handled poorly but this is exactly the type of question we need to ask in order to determine how to best develop our team member.

We need to know the direction that the team member is heading so that the development plan that we design has both reward and stretch in it and is therefore more likely to be actioned and more likely to yield tangible results for all concerned.

So we need to be able to ask that question in a way that will get the best possible response.

Two things will help here.

1. Pre-framing

   Notice the response people give if they have been asked this question and have not been able to answer it. Often you would hear something like . . . "I got asked that stupid question 'where do you see yourself in 5 years' time?' I don't know where I want to be in 5 years' time. I don't even know about next month let alone next 5 years. I hate that question, it is such a dumb question to ask."

   This sort of response indicates two things. A lack of ability to answer the question (I don't know) and a poor attitude around the question (I hate that question).

   Once again. Pre-framing to the rescue!

   Imagine that you catch up with the person you wish to develop in the corridor two days before your development meeting. To pre-frame the question, you might say something like . . .

   I wanted to catch up with you on Wednesday at 10 a.m. if that's OK. I just wanted to say thank you very much for the excellent work you have been putting in over the last couple of months.

I also wanted to give something back to you by way of saying thank you on behalf of myself and the organization. Now I wanted to make this as useful to you as possible so something that would help me is if you could think a little about where you're headed for in terms of your career or work and also in terms of outside of work. Hobbies, interests family etc. anything you can think of that is important to you really.

So I'd be curious to know what you would like to be doing more of or less of in the next few years or even if you have a clear idea of where you see yourself in the next 2–5 years because then we might be able to help you get there.

Then when it comes to the actual meeting and you ask "So what is going to become more important and less important for you over the next 2–5 years?" you are more likely to get something to work with.

2. Multiple Contexts

The other tool that will help you is to ask them to think about multiple contexts. Imagine how attached your best people are going to be to your organization and to you as a manager if you are able to help them achieve their hopes, dreams, and desires outside of work.

. . . if you could think a little about where you're headed for in terms of your career or work and also in terms of outside of work. Hobbies, interests family etc. anything you can think of that is important to you really.

The development plans that provide the biggest bang for your buck are the ones that develop people professionally and personally. This is where you can really contribute to your team members' sense of balance between work and their life outside of work.

Identify Development Tactics

Development tactics can be both professional and personal.

Professional Development

A trap for young players here is to look into your in-tray and find the project that has been hanging around your neck like the proverbial albatross and thinking that your team members' development is an excellent opportunity to get that project done and develop them at the same time.

Two words of warning here:

1. You have put your needs before your team members' needs and they will recognize "dumping" as quickly as you would.
2. Loading your best team member up with more work is no reward. If you are serious about how their performance has helped you then take something off them before you give the new responsibilities or tasks.

Professional development tactics

There are a number of tried and true methods of developing people professionally. These could include:

- Being a mentor
- Having a mentor
- Being a team coach
- Special projects
- Training courses
- Tertiary studies
- Cross-training
- Job sharing
- Field trips
- Study tours
- Research assignments
- Being the company's representative with industry bodies
- Site visits
- Job swapping
- Etc.

This list is by no means exhaustive. There are perhaps an infinite number of ways to develop a person. The skill is to select the appropriate tactic for the desired outcome.

What an exceptional manager would do is to identify what development needs the team member has and then select a task that will both develop those needs and benefit the business. They will also provide the resources (time, budget, equipment, and support) required to complete the new task or responsibility.

What follows is a tool that will prove invaluable with making these selections. It takes some generic competencies that you might be looking to develop and cross-references them with some development principles that will make the tactic selection much easier.

Personal Development

Often when people hear the phrase "personal development" they think of sensory deprivation training courses that starve you of the normal things in life like food, sunlight, and freedom of thought for a few days so you are more malleable and then ask you to take off all your clothes and hold hands to sing nude John Denver songs before walking over hot coals and making a fist, punching the air and yelling "YES" in some sort of positive anchor to your most resourced state.

What you didn't think of that? Oh! It must be me!

Professional development is usually done with the belief that there will be some direct positive impact on the business as well as the individual.

Personal development, in this context, is probably best described as any activity that will develop the individual for their sake and not directly for the organization's sake.

It is important to point out that some organizations are more open to non-mainstream methods of development than others. If you are unsure about what your organization is prepared to do for its team members, then ask. Keeping in mind, however, the best ways to ask.

Development tactics matrix	A task that will stretch them	Management of a team	Fix existing difficulties	Important assignment	Managing business diversity	Managing the businesses profile	Setting a new direction	New responsibilities	Persuasion & influence	Working in a project group	Putting your stamp on something	Right sizing	Start an initiative from scratch
Task Competencies:													
Autonomy	□	□	□	□	□		□	□			□		
Balance								□					
Decision-making	□		□	□	□		□	□			□		□
Persistence	□			□		□	□		□				□
Problem Solving			□	□			□	□	□				□
Systemic Thinking			□				□	□					□
People Competencies:													
Composure	□	□	□	□	□	□			□		□		□
Conflict Resolution		□	□	□	□				□		□	□	□
Dealing with Senior Staff	□	□	□	□	□		□	□	□		□	□	□
Empathy		□						□	□	□			
Flexibility	□			□			□	□					
Leading Others		□	□				□	□	□	□	□	□	□
Motivation		□	□				□	□	□		□	□	□
Negotiation				□	□	□	□	□	□			□	
Self-awareness	□							□		□			
Working as a Team		□							□				
Specific Technical Competencies:													
Technical Knowledge							□	□		□	□		
Business Knowledge				□			□	□	□	□			
Effective Use of Systems	□		□							□			

Would we be able to pay for Toni to do a 'Self Actualization Through Macramé' course?	*Versus*	"Toni has been a real powerhouse for us over the last 12–18 months. I figured that she has saved the organization over $500,000 with the streamlining and innovative ideas she has implemented. So I was wondering if the organization would be open to some innovative way of saying thank you to Toni?"

Some examples of personal development activities that I have known organizations to sponsor their team members through include:

- Learning to race motorcycles
- Time in a recording studio
- Access to financial planning
- Accounting advice
- Learning how to use a software application for a personal interest
- Art classes
- Physical fitness activities
- Sport team sponsorship
- Homeopathic and alternative medicine courses
- And yes the personal development courses

The more targeted you are to your team members' needs, the more loyalty you will engender.

Build the Development Plan

There are some minimal critical specifications to building a development plan:

1. **They are committed to hard copy or soft copy**
   Having a plan "in your head" isn't good enough. Committing it to hard or soft copy sends the message to your team member that you are serious about their development.
2. **SMART goals are identified**
   I have a goal. That is to be dirty rotten filthy stinkin' rich.
   This is not a SMART goal for several reasons.

a. Specific

First, I need to increase the level of specificity of the goal. What exactly do I mean by "dirty rotten filthy stinkin' rich?" Perhaps a more accurate phrase is "To be financially independent."

b. Measurable

Now I need to put a number in there somewhere. Make it quantifiable. How much would mean I was financially independent? Perhaps to have $2 million in income-producing assets.

There needs to be some sort of measure. Measuring someone's development fully objectively could be difficult. The aim is probably less about being fully objective and more about seeing tangible improvement.

With this in mind, the number could become something as simple as a self-administered survey of my level of skill, comfort, ease, happiness.

For example, before the development activities I would rate myself a 3/10 when it comes to knowing how to do X. After the development activities, I would like to rate myself an 8/10.

c. Attainable

The goal needs to be attainable. Both parties need to believe that the outcome is a stretch and possible nonetheless. If there is concern about the attainability of the goal, identify what aspects of the goal are negotiable and what is not negotiable.

To continue our example:

Not negotiable:

- Financially independent
- $2 million

Negotiable:

- Income-producing assets (perhaps I could include the house I live in)

d. Relevant

This is where you ensure that the goal is relevant to the team member you are wanting to develop. Does the goal suit their needs and wants? Does it link in to their bigger picture of where they see themselves in the future?

   e. Time Framed

The last component is to give the goal a deadline.

So our example now becomes:

"To be financially independent with $2 million worth of income-producing assets by December 20XX."

3. **Specific action steps listed**

For action steps, refer to the given development matrix and identify what steps are necessary to ensure the selected task happens. In my experience the more specific the action step, the more likely it is to happen.

For example, it is relatively difficult to "Implement a new Customer Relationship Management System (CRM)." It is, however, relatively simple to:

   a. Identify and contact others within the organization who have an interest in CRM

   b. Research similar organizations' CRM systems

   c. Research internal needs and idiosyncrasies when managing clients and client information

   d. Develop selection criteria

   e. Research the available CRMs

   f. Call for tenders from three providers who most match selection criteria etc. . . .

4. **Specific people are identified to be responsible for the completion of each step**

Here you are looking for someone to be responsible for the action being taken, not necessarily the person who will take the action.

5. **Milestones and deadlines are identified**

How many times have you set a task with a deadline only to find out just before the deadline falls due that the deadline will not be met?

It would be hard for a manager with any level of experience to answer "Nil" to that question.

The easiest way to ensure that a deadline will be met is to monitor progress with the use of mini deadlines or milestones. Remember that the level of the team members' skill will determine how far apart the milestones will need to be.

An Example Development Action Plan

Objective: To develop my ability to build persuasive business cases that are accepted by the senior management team with a hit rate of 75 percent or better by December 20XX.

Activity	Action Steps	By Who	By When
1. Coaching	i. Identify role model for building persuasive business cases	Mgr	10/02/XX
	ii. Approach for assistance and to act as coach/mentor	Mgr	12/02/XX
	iii. Discuss past cases and identify specific skills to develop	Mgr & TM	19/02/XX
	iv. Practice skills in mock situations	TM	5/03/XX
	v. Debrief the practice	TM	5/03/XX
2. Training	i. Identify appropriate training program	Mgr	5/03/XX
	ii. Contact referees to question quality of training	Mgr	12/03/XX
	iii. Develop learning objectives before attending	Mgr & TM	19/03/XX
	iv. Attend training	TM	30/04/XX
	v. Debrief training	Mgr & TM	30/04/XX
3. Build and present Case 1	i. Select issue to build a case around	Mgr & TM	30/04/XX
	ii. Plan the approach	TM	14/05/XX
	iii. Run past coach/mentor	TM	14/05/XX
	iv. Incorporate feedback	TM	21/05/XX
	v. Preliminary lobbying of senior management	Mgr & TM	4/06/XX
	vi. Present to senior management	TM	11/06/XX
	vii. Follow up and debrief	Mgr & TM	18/06/XX
4. Process improvement	i. Use feedback from case 1 to determine appropriate development activities	Mgr & TM	18/06/XX
5. Build and present Case 2	i. Select issue to build a case around	Mgr & TM	30/08/XX
	ii. Plan the approach	TM	14/09/XX
	iii. Run past coach/mentor	TM	14/09/XX
	iv. Incorporate feedback	TM	21/09/XX
	v. Preliminary lobbying of senior management	Mgr & TM	4/10/XX
	vi. Present to senior management	TM	11/10/XX
	vi. Follow up and debrief	Mgr & TM	18/10/XX

Implement the Development Plan

If you have ever had anything to do with development plans, it is easy to be cynical about them. This is often because no one is quite sure who is responsible for making them happen and so we assume it's the other person and so nothing happens.

If you wish to be an average manager then what you do is use phrases like:

"It is your development plan, so you are responsible for making this happen."

Not only is this is an abdication of your responsibility as a manager, it is also sending a very clear message to your team member about how much you really value them.

Yes, yes. I know. You did take the time to sit down with them and thank them for their efforts. You even put together this wonderful piece of bureaucratic paperwork called development plan. What more should you do?

Talk is cheap. How many leaders do you know who say one thing and then do another? What do you think about them?

> "Be what you want to see."

- An exceptional leader recognizes that actions speak louder than words and therefore they nominate themselves to complete some of the steps.
- Exceptional managers allocate the first two or three steps of the process to themselves to send a very clear message that this development plan will happen.
- Exceptional managers follow up the steps that their team members are responsible for making happen.

If you do, the message that your team members will get is that you take this seriously, you are prepared to put your money where your mouth is, you walk the talk, and you really do appreciate them, their efforts, and their value.

Monitor Progress

At this stage your role becomes one more of a coach/colleague as your team member is developing new skills, behaviors, and attitudes through activity. Some key skills for you to practice as discussed in the coaching chapter are:

- Providing balanced supportive feedback using the "EDI" method.
- Taking the team members beyond the current level of their thinking by asking "What else/what if" type questions.

CHAPTER 6

Counseling

When Does Counseling Work Best?

Now come on—be honest.

- Did you just jump to this part of the book because you want to know how to deal with that annoying team member?
- Are you reading this chapter in the hope that it will provide you with ammunition needed to sack the slack team member that is taking up so much of your time at work?
- Have you jumped to the conclusion that a certain team member needs counseling without doing the due diligence of objective performance analysis as described in the opening chapters?

If you answered yes to any of those questions, you will not find your answers here. Counseling works best when you have accurately and objective analyzed the performance of your team members and found them to be highly competent but not committed.

Low commitment could also be low commitment to the team or to the organization's values.

What Could Be Causing Low Commitment

I always find it wise to remind myself as to all the possible causes of a low commitment before I take action. Even though I may strongly believe that I know what is causing the low commitment, there have been a number of occasions when if I was a betting man I would have lost considerable amounts of money betting on what secrets people hide.

As well as the obvious issues:

- Boredom
- Being passed over for promotion
- Clash of personalities
- Lack of communication
- Inaccurate communication
- Lack of resources
- Staff cuts
- Restructuring
- Strong competition
- Poor product
- Poor systems
- Lack of leadership
- Clash in values
- Lack of skill
- Mismatch in expectations
- Lack of recognition

And this is not an exhaustive list of the issues that may exist within the work environment. Outside of work people become even less predictable:

- Relationship problems
- New relationship
- Family issues
- New addition to the family
- Problems with pets
- Becoming aware of sexual preferences
- Illness—self, family, friends
- Sport representation
- Hobbies
- Purchasing a home
- Finding a place to rent

Good or bad, big or small, people's commitment to work can be reduced for many reasons. Truth is stranger than fiction and any manager who thinks that they have seen it all is in for a big surprise.

How to Improve Commitment

There are probably two extremes of corporate counseling that you may have experienced at some stage. They are:

Aggressive counseling:
Aggressive counseling might sound something like this . . .

You! Yes you know who I'm talking to. Don't play the innocent shy boy with me. I want you in my office now! You have a problem and the problem is your attitude. I want to know what you are going to do about it. Because I'm telling you that I've had just about enough of your incompetence and you are on thin ice. So, it's either clean up your act or on your bike. Well which is it?

Psychoanalysis counseling:
Psychoanalysis counseling might sound something like this . . .

Manager: "So when did all this start?"

Team Member: "Well it all started when I was 3. My Father wouldn't take me to the circus. I was a fragile child who had a thing for clowns and I just couldn't handle that sort of rejection . . ."

As we would be foolish to assume what is causing the low commitment, perhaps a good middle ground to start off with is "Cause identification counseling." Cause identification counseling could be defined as "To identify what is causing the low commitment and then determine whether you need to be slightly more issue focused or whether to be more individual focused."

How to Open the Counseling Conversation

Imagine the following scenario:
You have been under a bit of pressure at home recently. It could be financial, relationship, health, commitments, family. All in all imagine that you are feeling quite stressed and have been for the last 3 weeks.

Your manager calls you in and says the following. Note your response:

I just wanted to talk to you about your performance over the last
3 weeks. You have been making some silly errors and as a result you
have cost us dearly. You have also been causing a lot of conflict in
the office and people have told me that they just can't talk to you
anymore as you are always at their throat and you explode at the
smallest issue. You have also been a little slack time-wise recently
and you are just plain not performing. I want to know what your
problem is and what you are going to do to get things back on track.

In the space below write down what you would be thinking/feeling at
this point in the conversation and how likely you would be to volunteer
what is currently happening outside of work.

Now compare your response to this:
Imagine the same scenario:
You have been under a bit of pressure at home recently. It could be
financial, relationship, health, commitments, family. All in all imagine
that you are feeling quite stressed and have been for the last 3 weeks.
This time your manager calls you in and says the following:

Thanks for coming in Rhonda. I just wanted to start by saying
that I can remember a time about 6 months ago when we were
working on that project together. Everyone was telling us that

there was no way that we would be able to complete that project on time or within the budget. But I think it was because of the creative ideas that you came up with for the implementation that meant that not only did we bring the project in on time but it was massively under budget. Once again thanks very much for that. That was a first class job.

Recently I've noticed a few things. I've noticed that there has been an increase in errors where I have not seen errors for ages. I have also noticed an increased tension in the office and I have also noticed a preference to arrive at work a little late and leave work on or before 5 p.m. when we used to still see each other around the corridors at 6 p.m.

So I'm thinking to myself that this is not the Rhonda that I'm used to working with.

And I'm feeling a little confused.

And what I would like is to get performance back to the level we had 6 months ago because that was great stuff.

So Have I got the whole picture? Is there something I'm missing?"

In the following space write down what you would be thinking/feeling at this point in the conversation and how likely you would be to volunteer what is currently happening outside of work.

In order to increase the likelihood that we identify the real cause of the low commitment, we will need to be very careful and deliberate in the way we start the conversation. Our opening remarks could set the scene for a defensive, aggressive, submissive, or constructive response.

The second example is the example we will use to identify the principles behind a good opening statement when trying to identify the cause of low commitment.

You and I

Often when people are asked to note what they are thinking or feeling in the first example, they describe the manager as being accusatory and blaming without knowing the cause of the issue. They note that their response would probably be defensive, aggressive, or submissive.

The main word that causes this response is the word "you."

As soon as we use the word "you" in this context, we are blaming the person for the results. We are playing the player and not the ball. We are blaming the individual and ignoring the task.

Now I can understand that you might be thinking something like "Yeah. That's lovely Rod; however, what if it is the person that is stuffing up?"

To which my response is: You cannot be certain why the person is stuffing up. Truth is stranger than fiction and while it might be convenient for us to think that it's just that they are useless, that is an expensive, often inaccurate, usually emotional and potentially dangerous, belief to have.

Approaching counseling with that belief can, and often does, lead to:

- ugly scenes in offices
- damage to your reputation as a manager
- the high cost of sacking and replacing the person in comparison to what could be the cheap alternative of performance improvement
- unfair dismissal cases

It also often hides an inability on behalf of the manager to deal with the issue effectively.

You might also be thinking "Ok Rod. So you telling me I have to deliver some feedback and I can't use the word 'you.' How do you deliver feedback without using 'you?'

You use the word 'I'.

If you think about it. When using the word 'you' in this context, you are making a judgment as to what is true for the other person. You have no right to do that. You will never know what is true for another person unless you spend years living with them. And even then . . .

When you use the word 'I' in this context, you are saying what is true for you. You have every right to do this.

Start with a Positive

Thanks for coming in Rhonda. I just wanted to start by saying that I can remember a time about 6 months ago when we were working on that project together. Everyone was telling us that there was no way that we would be able to complete that project on time or within the budget. But I think it was because of the creative ideas that you came up with for the implementation that meant that not only did we bring the project in on time but it was massively under budget. Once again thanks very much for that. That was a first class job.

Now the more cynical of you might be thinking "Oh right. Here we go. The good old sandwich technique." Tell them something nice so you lull them into a false sense of security and then hit them with the ugly bits and then finish on a high afterward. This is rubbish. People see right through it. If you try to start with something positive, they will just be waiting for the "*However.*" And, on top of that, starting with the positive is unnecessary padding and beating around the bush.

There are a number of valid concerns there; let's look at them one at a time.

1. *The good old sandwich technique. Tell them something nice so you lull them into a false sense of security and then hit them with the ugly bits and then finish on a high afterward.*

   There are very important reasons why it is useful to start with some positive feedback.

   - Starting on a positive note dramatically reduces defensiveness. Less defensiveness means a greater chance of identifying and working with the real issue

   - It shows you are aware of the team member's total performance and you are not getting things out of proportion and that you are not just nit-picking this particular incident in isolation

   - It provides a contrast between desired behavior and current behavior. This is a very persuasive technique that reduces the chance of endless debate about the accuracy of your observations. It also makes your case almost undeniable.

   Advertising people have understood the power of contrast and used it well. Think of the advertisements for losing weight. They have a before and an after picture next to each other. The after picture is only persuasive because they have the before picture to contrast it against. If there was only an after picture, you might think something like "I bet she was born like that!" or "I bet he's always had a 6-pack." This becomes undeniable when we have a before picture to contrast it with. Even though the person has had a complete makeover, are now in color and have been fitted out in slimming clothes . . .

   You can do this contrast verbally by starting with feedback about when they exhibited the sorts of behaviors that you want to see.

   Some people ask at this stage, "But what if they have never exhibited any positive behaviors?" There are a couple of responses to this question:

   i. Why are they still working for you?

   ii. If you cannot find any redeeming qualities of this person then you may be too emotional to deliver the feedback at this stage. Providing feedback in a constructive manner requires a degree of disassociation (i.e., to not be overly concerned about the counseling or the outcome).

When negotiating something, say to purchase a house or car, the more emotionally attached you are to the outcome, the less your power to create it. The less attached to the outcome, the more powerful you are in the negotiation.

A similar dynamic happens in providing feedback to people. So I would recommend, as much as possible, to wait until you have cooled down a little, get some perspective on the issue, and realize that there is more to life than performance management.

- A final reason which we will discuss later when we look at the final component of the opening message in counseling.

1. *If you try to start with something positive, they will just wait for the "However."*
   - They will be if that is your intention. Your vocal tone and your body language will give you away. If it is your intention to just start off with a positive because it recommended that you do so in a book, then that will come through. Just like you can tell when someone is not being genuine with you.

     The performance management version of this is, "If you can't start a counseling session with something nice, either you should be well past counseling and more toward termination of services or don't do the counseling until you have the ability to provide genuine, positive, and specific feedback."

     > As my mother would say, "If you can't say anything nice don't say anything at all!" On ya Mum!

   - Don't use "However." Don't use "although" and don't use "but." These words are used when you want to express two potentially opposing ideas in one sentence. You do not want to do that. There is no need and it will only do more harm than good when you have gone to the trouble of saying something positive and then you discount it by saying "however."

You have finished expressing one idea and now want to express a different one. So separate the statements. Full stop, new paragraph, capital letter. You may even pause in between the completion of the positive and the commencement of the observations you have made of their performance.

2. *And on top of that, starting with the positive is unnecessary padding and beating around the bush.*

- Once again . . . If that is your intention then that is how it will come across. Using the same argument as the gun lobbyists use . . . it is not the gun that kills, it is the intention of the user of the gun that kills.

  Same with this stuff. It is not the tool that is manipulative, insincere, or padded; if, however, it is your intention to manipulate, be insincere, or to pad, then it is your intention that we should call into question, not the tool.

- Agreed that there are some team members who either prefer the direct approach or will best understand if they receive the direct approach. For these team members you can speed this up.

How about this . . .

"Thanks for coming in Rhonda. I just wanted to start by saying that I can remember 6 months ago when we were working on that project. Everyone was saying 'Impossible, can't be done, give up now.' Then along came Rhonda. New ideas, new approach lots of experience. As a result we saved $1.5M. Once again thanks very much for that. That was a first class job.

Recently I've noticed a few things. I've noticed that there has been an increase in errors, an increased tension in the office and a preference to arrive at work a little late and leave work a little early.

So I'm thinking that this is not the Rhonda I'm used to working with. I'm feeling a little confused and what I would like is to get performance back to the level we had 6 months ago.

So Have I got the whole picture? Is there something I'm missing?"

Timed from beginning to end, including pauses and intonation, this only takes about 45 to 50 seconds.

Out of the Front Door (OTFD)

After starting with a positive, we need to provide the contrast and state what we have *observed*, what we are *thinking*, how we are *feeling*, and what we *desire* or what we would like.

Observed
Think
Feel
Desire

So we have the process called OTFD.

OTFD can also stand for "Out The Front Door." Which is how you might feel after the team member has done what they have done. You might feel like taking them out the front door, you hold them and I'll hit them!

Let that be your trigger to remember that you need to use the word "I" instead of "you" and to structure your message using OTFD.

Let's look at the second part of the message with OTFD in mind:

Recently I've **observed** a few things. I've noticed that there has been an increase in errors where I have not seen errors for ages. I have also noticed an increased tension in the office and I have also noticed a preference to arrive at work a little late and leave work on or before 5 p.m. when we used to still see each other around the corridors at 6 p.m.

So I'm **thinking** to myself that this is not the Rhonda that I'm used to working with.

And I'm **feeling** a little confused.

And what I would like (No one says 'What I **desire** . . .' It just fits the OTFD thing) is to get performance back to the level we had 6 months ago because that was great stuff.

Observed

There are two important points here:

1. Remember to avoid using the word "you." Yes, it is difficult. No, it is not impossible. What will make it easier is if you use the word "I" and the statement "I have noticed . . ." or "I have observed . . ."
2. Be objective. Avoid emotional value judgments or qualitative judgments that could be debated. What will help is if you have used the "Behavior Description Generator" to identify objective behaviors to describe performance.

Avoid	Use
"You are causing lots of fights in the office"	"I have noticed an increased tension in the office"
"You have been starting late and leaving early"	"I have noticed a preference to start work late and leave early"
"You have been making some silly errors recently"	"I have noticed some errors where there has not been errors for some time"
"You have been rude to customers"	"I have seen the phone slammed down at the end of conversations"
"You have been displaying a poor attitude"	"I have noticed a rolling of eyes, a folding of arms, and a shaking of head in meetings when people make suggestions"
"You have not communicated very well with the other staff"	"I have noticed that communication on last week's decision was one way. There was no listening or acknowledgement that others' comments were considered"
"You are an oxygen thief and while you might be the full six pack you lack the little plastic thingy that holds it all together"	"I have noticed that our supply of oxygen has been more quickly used than in the past and I have also noticed that the 6 pack bottles are separate"

Sometimes people ask "What happens if the team members say 'Are you talking about me?'"

There are often two reasons why someone would ask this question at this point:

1. They are making the connection between the stated behaviors and their behaviors and are honestly looking for confirmation.
2. They are baiting you to fight back, lose your cool, and provide them with a reason to walk out or fight back.

Either way your response would be the same. Simply say "Yes." And continue as planned. The "Yes" will confirm the link for those needing the confirmation and will not provide the fighters with sufficient reason to increase their anger levels or walk out.

The baiting people are looking to start a pattern that will allow them to legitimately get out of the situation. The pattern is: I bait you, you bite (an emotive response), I use the bite as a reason to raise the stakes with an equally emotional response to your bite. You bite back harder, I bite back harder, you start yelling and being unreasonable, I walk out blaming you for my behaviors.

Do not start this pattern. Stay reasonable. Stay unemotional. Stay detached and you will be powerful.

Think

Let them know what you think when you observe those behaviors:
   "I'm thinking to myself that . . .

- this is not the Rhonda I'm used to working with"
- this is not what was discussed at the beginning of this appraisal period/beginning of this year"
- this is not the sorts of behaviors that will achieve the results the team is aiming for"
- this will make our work more difficult than it needs to be"
- this could result in increased absenteeism and 1 day sickies"

Just one will do. Too many will freak them out and is probably overkill.

Once again, avoid emotional words and subjectivity:
"I'm thinking to myself that . . .

- this is unfair and selfish"
- this is just plain laziness"
- this has got to stop"
- this light an unstoppable wick to a retribution the likes of which we have not seen in our life time"

Feel

Let them know how you feel when you think that:
"So I'm feeling . . .

- a little concerned"
- a little confused"
- a little unsure"
- a little worried"
- a little anxious"

Just one will do. Too many will freak them out and is probably overkill.
Once again, avoid overly emotional words:
"So I'm feeling . . .

- really really angry"
- like I'm about to explode"
- like I'm at the end of my patience"
- severely let down"
- like my mother did when she found the Playboy magazine and bong I had hidden in the space under my lowest drawer"

Desire

Reset the standard of performance you would like to see.
"What I would like:

- is to get performance back to the level we had 6 months ago"
- is to have the error rate below 1 percent"

- is to work in an office where people have a good productive and enjoyable working relationship"
- is to work with a team of people who take their work but not themselves too seriously"
- is to work out a way of ensuring that we meet our targets"
- is to ensure that as much as possible people want to come to work because they are getting more out of it than just a pay packet and a headache"

And here is the other reason that we need to start the counseling conversation with something positive. Because when we get to the "What I would like . . ." bit of the conversation we can link back to the positive behaviors that we have seen them exhibit in the past and we know they are competent to do.

Ask a Question

Now we need to prompt a response. We need to hear from them. We have stated our case and we now need to hear what is going on in their mind or in their heart.

As a general rule of thumb, a question with the word "I" in it will work better than a question with the word "you" in it.

For example:

Avoid	Use
"So what is your problem?"	"So have I got the whole picture?"
"Is there something you want to tell me?"	"So is there something I'm missing in all of this?"
"What are you going to do about it?"	"So is there something I don't understand?"

Possible Responses to This Conversation

Please remember how you said you would respond to this statement when we asked you to note your response at the beginning of this chapter. Most people will respond in a manner that will allow you to solve the issue as best you can.

And then there will be the minority, the tough nuts, the difficult responses. There are a number of responses that could fall into this category:

The Denial

"No. Everything's fine. It's all good. No problem really."

The Blamer

"Well I'm glad you brought it up. It's about time someone did something with the other team members. They are impossible to work with. And the computer system. Well that came out of the Ark. How are we expected to process customer orders when the system crashes every other day. And until those drop kicks in management get their act together and realize what we have to put up with around here . . ."

The Justification

"Look. I know I should be doing it the new way, but I'm going to stick to the old way a little longer just until all the bugs are ironed out. Then I'll switch over."

The Quitter

"That's it. I've had enough. I am sick to death of being the scapegoat around here. I'm not going to do anything extra anymore. From here on in I'm only going to do exactly what is asked of me and no more."

These are what we might call "poor responses."

Principles for Dealing with Poor Responses

No matter what the poor responses are, a clever manager will operate under some key principles:

1. Feeling versus thinking
2. Pace before you lead
3. What I need is . . .

Feeling versus Thinking

If you have ever had any experience in dealing with customer complaints, you will know that it is good practice to listen, not interrupt and allow the customer to "get it of their chest." You will know that if they are interrupted or if we try to offer a solution before they have had their say that it will most likely make the customer even more upset, the solution will be lost in the emotion of the moment and it will make it twice as difficult to reach a satisfactory agreement for both parties.

Why is this the case?

Well, to speak metaphorically, most of us have a seesaw operating inside of us. We are either thinking or we are feeling. While we are able to switch from one to the other in a split second, one tends to operate at the expense of the other.

So when the customer is complaining, they are "feeling" and therefore not really "thinking" too clearly. So if we offer a solution while they are still "feeling," we are more likely to make matters worse. We need to deal with the feeling component first and then the customer will be more open to a logical solution.

So a clever customer service representative knows how to allow the customer to "get it of their chest" without interruption and with support . . .

"Oh really," "Is that right," "No wonder you are upset," "That must have been so frustrating."

Then the customer will reach a point in the conversation when they have finished "getting it off their chest." This will be punctuated with something. A statement or a gesture that indicates that they have finished and are now awaiting a response from you.

"So. I want to know what we do now!" "Anyway . . ." "So I want you to fix this before I leave."

You would do well then to recognize that while the customer is not totally ready to think about a solution yet, they are ready to start up their thinking side and slowly shut down the feeling side. A couple of simple questions on behalf of the customer service representative would help this transition.

"Now what day was that phone conversation?" "Do you have your account number?" "Do you remember if it was X or Y?"

Just a simple question will do. The aim here is to assist with the transition from feeling to thinking. In order to answer these questions, the customer needs to switch on their brains and in order to switch on their brains they need to shut down their feelings.

After they have answered these questions, they are going to be far more open to thinking about a solution.

The same is true with first responses to feedback. Often the person is responding emotionally and just wants to "get it of their chest." Our role here is to listen empathically, and not to impose or even approach solutions until the emotional heat is gone and the logic has returned.

This also holds true if the team member starts to cry (No guys, this is not just a tactic that women employ to put you off your game).

I have seen all types of people cry for all types of reasons. What I notice happens is that if you stick with them through the tears, offer them tissues or a cup of tea/coffee, their level of trust in you dramatically increases. Their level of respect for you as a manager and as a person increases dramatically and because you have shared something with them that they have not shared with all of their work colleagues, you will find yourself in a box seat to identify a way of truly assisting someone through a difficult time, making a friend for life as well as improving performance.

How do you do this?

1. Listen and support
2. Wait for the signal
3. Ask simple questions

Pace before You Lead

How do you have an argument?

Well if you have ever watched and listened to two or more people having an argument, chances are you may have noticed some key words and behaviors that indicate quite clearly that things are becoming heated.

These could include:

- Pointing of fingers
- Raised voices
- Shaking of heads
- Expletives
- Folding of arms
- Defensive/aggressive postures.

There are also three words that almost go unnoticed and without them it is very difficult to have an argument. The words are:

- No
- Yes, but . . .

If you think about it, what these words do is to show that your listening has been a façade. That you are not really listening, you are just waiting for your turn to talk.

These words also discount what has just been said and in doing so will increase the likelihood that their next response will be more defensive or even more aggressive.

Sometimes it is fun to have an argument. A good verbal stoush with good friends can be challenging, interesting, and fun. And there are other times when an argument is not useful. Think of all the times when you would like to not have an argument. Think of all of the situations when agreement has been more important than victory, that the relationship has been more important than accuracy, that the flow of conversation has been more important than proving your intelligence.

In these situations the words "No" and "Yes, but . . ." will be of less use.

Try replacing them with "Yes . . . And . . ."

If you just say "Yes, and what you haven't thought of is . . ." then you might as well not bother. The use of "Yes . . . And . . ." requires a little more sophistication than that.

What you are doing here is two things.

First we are "pacing" the other person's opinion/position. We do this by finding some part of what it is that they said that we:

- Agree with
- Acknowledge

- Accept
- Can see
- Have also noticed
- And if all else fails . . . Can understand.

And then we add to that our position, our beliefs, our perspective. Here's how it sounds:

"No" "Yes, but . . ."	"Yes . . . (pace) . . . And . . . (lead) . . ."
"Yeah, but AFL is just 'kill the dill with the pill', there is no skill in that." "No, that is not true. There is a lot of skill in AFL. You try and kick the ball the length they do with the accuracy they do. That ain't easy." "No. Anyone with ½ a brain can do that. But you try get the ball past 11 other people using only your feet. That is skill!"	"AFL is just 'kill the dill with the pill', there is no skill in that." "Yes you are right. There is little skill in 'kill the dill with the pill' and AFL has many other aspects to the game than the tackle component. To be a top player you need to be able to kick the ball far and accurately. That takes skill." "Yes kicking the ball the lengths they do with the accuracy they do is impressive and being able to get a ball past 11 other players using only your feet is pure magic."
"Men are better drivers than women because it has been shown in tests that men have a superior spatial capacity and can therefore calculate distances and speed much better than women." "Yes, but why is it more expensive to insure a car if the main driver is male and under 25 than if the main driver is female? The insurance companies know that most accidents involve males." "No. Most of the accidents that are reported might involve males but that doesn't include the millions of little car park and less than 10 km per hour type accidents that women are famous for."	"Men are better drivers than women because it has been shown in tests that men have a superior spatial capacity and can therefore calculate distances and speed much better than women." "Yes, I have heard of tests that show that men do have a bit of an advantage when it comes to spatial awareness and what I noticed is that it more expensive to insure a car if the main driver is male and under 25 than if the main driver is female. The insurance companies know that most accidents involve males." "Yes, that is true. Most insurance companies will charge a premium for male drivers under 25 and what those figures might not include is the little car park and less than 10 km per hour type accidents."

"No. It's all good. There is no problem." "No, that is not true. There is a problem. That is the problem I have just highlighted to you regarding the conflict in the office, the late starts and the error rates." "Yes, but that is because the managers in IT couldn't get their act together to fix the system when we needed it." "No it was nothing to do with the system. The problem was with the person using the system. The system works fine." "Well it didn't that day."	"No. It's all good. There is no problem." "Yes, things by and large are going well. We look like we will meet our targets as a team and most of us will receive a bonus. And there are some issues that will mean not everyone receives a bonus. They are teamwork, punctuality and error rates." "Yes, but that is because the managers in IT couldn't get their act together to fix the system when we needed it." "Yes, I agree that IT are a little slow to act sometimes and the issues we are addressing here are ongoing ones and ones that exist outside of the system that we use."
"Look. I know what you're saying. I should be doing it the new way, but I'm going to stick to the old way a little longer just until all the bugs are ironed out. Then I'll switch over." "No, that is not an option. We are all supposed to be using the new system as of last month." "Yes, but the new system sucks. Everyone knows it. I'm just the only one brave enough to do something about it." "Yes, but what you're doing is making things worse in the long run."	"Look. I know what you're saying. I should be doing it the new way, but I'm going to stick to the old way a little longer just until all the bugs are ironed out. Then I'll switch over." "Yes there are some very annoying bugs that need to ironed out in order to make the process as efficient as it could be. And we need to know what those bugs are, and the best way to find those bugs is to use the system in real life situations and see what happens." "Yes, but the new system sucks. Everyone knows it. I'm just the only one brave enough to do something about it." "Yes you are being brave and what will be the most useful way of dealing with this for the team is to have everyone identifying what the difficulties are and then working with the project managers to iron out the bugs."

Yes, I can understand that this may initially sound a little contrived, even a little conciliatory and if you can recognize the benefit of remaining calm and in control during a potentially volatile situation, here is the tool to help you.

Yes, I can see that this may be difficult when you first try to do it in conversation and if you persist with it, like all skills, you will be able to dramatically reduce the level of needles conflict in your life, increase your level of control in difficult situations, and increase the likelihood that you are dealing with the real issue and not a defensive response. Best of all, with practice you will be able to do this effectively, effortlessly, and seamlessly.

What I Need Is . . .

Remember that the final line in all of this is that it is your responsibility as a manager to ensure that certain performance standards are met. So no matter where the conversation goes, you can bring it back to the reason for having the conversation, which is the "Desire" component of the OTFD

> "Play the ball . . . not the person."

message . . . "What I would like . . ." It is about the issue, not about the person.

Where to End the Counseling Conversation

The aim of the counseling conversation is most likely twofold:

1. To identify what is causing the low levels of commitment.

    We have talked a lot about how to start the conversation and we now recognize the importance reducing defensive/aggressive responses and increasing the likelihood that we are dealing with the real issue, not a cover-up. We have also spent some time over tactics for the least desirable responses. Now we need to know when to stop the counseling conversation.

2. To agree on a plan to improve commitment.

    The counseling conversation ends when a plan has been agreed upon.

    The actions in the plan are as diverse as the reasons for low commitment and might include time off to deal with personal issues or access to an employee assistance program.

    A word of warning . . . Avoid rewarding low commitment!

    In the late 1980s to early 1990s, organizations "discovered" rightsizing. Rightsizing is, of course, the politically correct term for terminating people's employment in an effort to reduce costs.

What happened in a lot of organizations is a redundancy culture was created.

Let's say that you work with someone called Narelle. Let's say that Narelle is deadwood in the organization. She is difficult to work with, she has been in the organization for years, she is coasting toward retirement, and has a very low commitment for anything the company says or does.

Organizations saw rightsizing as an opportunity to make the Narelles of this world redundant. So they paid Narelle a ridiculous sum of guilt money, offered her some very expensive counseling, and waved goodbye with tear in their eyes and tongue in their cheek.

Narelle, after the initial shock, uses this newfound wealth to pay off the mortgage, goes on a trip overseas, and upon return finds a job with either the same or a rival organization as a "contractor" earning twice as much as she did previously.

Narelle phones you up and says "Honestly, it was the best thing that ever happened to me. I've paid of the mortgage, I've travelled extensively and now I'm working again earning more than I ever dreamed."

As you are listening to this, a message arrives telling you that the company is considering a second round or redundancies. You start thinking that this redundancy thing is a good thing, so in order to increase your chances that "your job" is selected to be made redundant. You start to behave just like Narelle did before she left. Now the organization has a team full of people who are behaving like deadwood. They are difficult to work with, they are coasting toward retirement, and show a very low commitment for anything the company says or does.

If, when trying to increase commitment levels you reward the person by promoting them, changing their responsibilities, developing them etc., you may be creating a counseling culture. A culture where your team members see that the way to get rewarded is to exhibit low commitment.

Clearly establish the behaviors that you want to stop and the behaviors that you want to increase before they are to be rewarded.

So the counseling conversation is ended when you have an agreement to take action that will result in increased commitment levels.

Whether or not you record the agreement in an action plan type arrangement will depend on the severity of the issue and the reasons for the lack of commitment. A good manager will recognize when the relationship is more important than the issue and vice versa. A poor manager will just do the same thing (either with an action plan or rely on verbal agreement) every time.

CHAPTER 7

Reassigning

Alternatives to Sacking

As we mentioned in Chapter 3 when we first introduced the idea of reassigning . . .

It is easy to jump to the conclusion that we should sack this person and hire someone else to do the job.

This is an expensive decision. It would cost an organization far more in both dollar costs and intangible costs to terminate an employment and find a new employee than it often does working with the person to determine what alternatives are available.

Remember, it could be that the team member is fantastic at other more important parts of their job than just this one area that they don't know how to do and don't want to learn.

Alternatives to sacking include:

- give the task to someone else
- determine if the task can be done by computer or other machinery
- have an external organization do the work
- hire a contractor or consultant
- ask, "What would happen if this task was not done?" Would it really matter?
- find them a job in the organization where their skills are suitable.

A good manager will be able to use a situation like this to find new and creative ways of improving their team's output through reassignment.

What Do I Do If All Else Fails?

It was Friday afternoon, 2.50 p.m., and I was in 5th class at school. Our teacher, Mr. Watson, said, "OK. I want you to rule up a new page." Do you remember having to rule up new pages? A margin in red down the left side and a line across the top of the page so the teacher could write comments after we had handed in the work.

> **"Once. OK everybody makes mistakes. Twice is sloppy, but three times is unacceptable."**

Now at 2.50 p.m. on a Friday the last thing you want to be doing is ruling up a new page. So I was not really concentrating too hard. As a result I misruled the margin and top line three times. Three big messy red marks across and down my page.

Mr. Watson looked over my shoulder and said, "Rod Matthews! What on earth is that? Once. OK everybody makes mistakes. Twice is sloppy, but three times is unacceptable."

Three strikes and you're out. A good rule for many things. I believe in most cases it is the same with team members.

If an incident or behavior happens once . . . OK everybody makes mistakes. Twice is sloppy. There is no excuse for three times. An exceptional manager would operate under the same premise.

In Australia there continues to be a lot of controversy about unfair dismissal laws. People claim that they make life unfairly difficult for small business. I would say that the laws are there to raise the standard of management. To ensure that managers treat their team members fairly. So if you are complaining about the unfair dismissal laws, I would ask you to take a long hard look at your skills as a manager.

It is with this in mind that I recommend the following process when counseling does not change performance.

1. Counseling #1
2. Counseling #2
3. Oral Warning
4. Documented Counseling #1 (Written warning)

5. Documented Counseling #2 (Written warning)
6. Termination of Services.

How to Stay Out of the Unfair Dismissal Courts

You will dramatically reduce the chance of ending up in the unfair dismissal courts if you do three things:

1. Use the behavior description generator to accurately identify the micro behaviors that are effecting performance
2. Follow the process outlined below
3. Obtain professional advice on or before step 3 "Oral Warning."

Counseling #1

This is as discussed in Chapter 6.

You would be wise to mark the meeting in your diary. Dependent on the severity of the issue you may choose to keep notes to include details in any performance appraisal system your company might use.

I would try to avoid this if I could as I believe that if you note the first time someone makes a mistake and include it in their performance appraisal, you are sending the message that errors are not tolerated. This may sound good initially and what it tends to lead to is a group of people who are reluctant to do anything from fear of being wrong and being caught out.

I prefer to operate by the adage "It is Ok to make mistakes. It is not Ok to not try."

Counseling #2

This is also as discussed in Chapter 6. This time you might want to begin to up the ante a little by including something like "This is the second time we have had to talk about this so I'm really keen to ensure that there is not a third conversation about the same behaviors."

Once again you would be wise to mark the meeting in your diary. Dependent on the severity of the issue you may choose to keep notes to include details in any performance appraisal system your company might use.

Oral Warning

It is now the third time that the behaviors have been noted. This is the time to draw the line in the sand and make it perfectly clear to the team member what the consequences will be if performance is not improved.

At this stage you may want to contact the Human Resources team in you organization or your manager just to talk through the situation. You can enlist their help if you feel you need it or you can do the oral warning yourself.

Either way, ensure the meeting is marked in your diary, note the reason for the meeting, the result of the meeting and any issues that you believe are wise to note.

This is where it is critical to be unattached to any outcome. Remember, the less attached to the outcome you are, the more control or power over the process you have.

Here is an example of the way to start the conversation. As you say this or your own opening statements be:

- Direct
- Calm
- Focused on performance improvement

As you know we have met now on two previous occasions to discuss the issues of:
  i. Punctuality
  ii. Error rates and
  iii. Teamwork

The level of performance that is required for these key expectations in this position are:
  i. To be available for our clients between the hours of 8.30 a.m. and 5 p.m.
  ii. Error rates below X percent
  iii. Behaviors consistent with good teamwork

The level of performance that I have noticed now on three separate occasions is:
  i. Arriving after 8.30 a.m. and packing up at 4.45 p.m.
  ii. Error rates is above X percent
  iii. There has recently been another yelling match in the office.

There is a large gap between the performance that is expected and the performance that I'm seeing. It is my role, as manager, to close this gap. There is one of two ways I can do that.

   i. I can improve the performance of the current incumbent or
   ii. I can replace the current incumbent with someone who is able to provide me with the level of performance I need.

Now I do not want to head down path ii and I don't think you do either. Nonetheless, this is now the third occasion that we have needed to discuss this performance. So rest assured that if performance slips to unacceptable levels after today's meeting, we will be heading down path ii.

Now we have tried "X" after our first meeting and we tried "Y" after our second meeting. Neither of them seemed to work. So, once again I ask the question: What needs to happen in order to get performance to acceptable levels.

In my experience, and in conversations with hundreds of other managers, if you have completed the first three steps well then 9 out of 10 people will improve their performance. Often because they are so shocked that someone has actually called their game and is preparing to play hardball if necessary.
Once again:

- Direct
- Calm
- Focused on performance improvement

Documented Counseling #1

In the approximately one out of 10 cases where performance doesn't improve, you will need to complete the necessary requirements to stay out of the unfair dismissal courts. If you have a Human Resources function in your organization, contact them as they are the experts in exactly this sort of thing.

If you do not have a Human Resource team then contact one of the many employer organizations that provide advice, products, and services in this area.

- Australian Human Resource Institute
- Australian Institute of Managers
- Your state or local Chamber of Commerce
- Your state or local Chamber of Manufacturers
- Or you could call a great consultant!!!

Rather than provide you with a standard approach to dealing with documented counseling, I would again direct you to the relevant experts because little knowledge could be a dangerous thing.

What I can do is recommend you keep in mind something we learned in Chapter 2. In an unfair dismissal court, you will be laughed at if you go in there with labels or value judgments. You will be dramatically increasing the likelihood that you win any legal action if you have clearly documented behaviors.

Documented Counseling #2

There have been quite a number of situations that I have heard of where team members leave, resign, and even disappear from the face of the earth before getting to this stage. They know the gig is up. They see that you have done everything by the book. They just want to avoid the nasty bits.

Termination of Services

This is at most a 5-minute meeting. If performance is still unsatisfactory at this stage then the decision is made to terminate services. If the decision has been made, then there is no need to drag it out with conversation, incriminations, blaming, and so on.

Five minutes' noting that performance has not improved as requested. Retaining all company property and arranging transport home.

If trust is part of the issue then escorting them on the premises is recommended. If trust is not part of the issue then it should be Ok for them to return to their desk momentarily to reclaim personal effects.

Once again, talk to the experts before tackling this one.

It's Not Always That Tough

What I have outlined above is the most that you would ever have to do. There are a number of things that would lead to instant dismissal. For example, stealing from the company or other team members, severe cases of sexual harassment, dishonesty, breach of contract.

Something that often makes this process tougher than it is expected to be is how managers deal with fluctuating performance. The scenario goes that the team member's performance improved after being counseled. Then out of the blue about 6 months down the track, the team member starts exhibiting the same behaviors.

A mistake is to start the process from scratch. If the team member has performed poorly on two occasions, it doesn't matter how far apart they are, it is the second occasion and should be a counseling #2.

I have heard of a number of cases where managers are going crazy dealing with a team member who momentarily improves performance long enough to get the manager to start the process afresh.

CHAPTER 8

Establishing a Direction

What makes the difference?

An undisputed timeless classic in management literature would be *Think and Grow Rich* by Napoleon Hill. In this astounding book, Hill interviews some of the most exceptional people in recent history: Henry Ford, John D. Rockefeller, Alexander Graham Bell, just to name a few. All of these peoples' experiences point to the idea that there are four main components to exceptional performance.

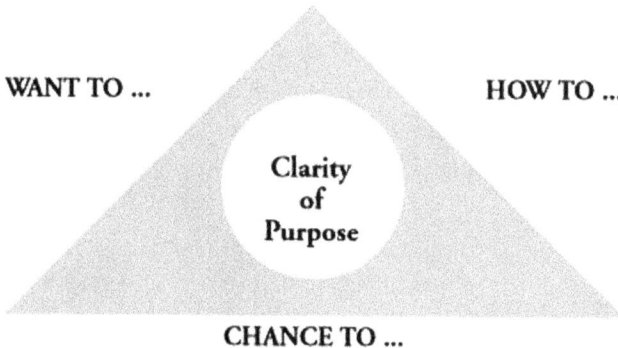

WANT TO ...   **HOW TO ...**

Clarity
of
Purpose

CHANCE TO ...

Want to . . . the Passion

One of the components to achieving significant results is that you need to want to . . . want to with a passion.

Now I can understand that you might be thinking, "So far so good. This is easy. I want to be rich. I want to have money to burn. And make no mistake Rod, I want it with a passion."

The thing is that you have to "want to" enough to do what it will take to create that wealth. Many of us want to do or have or be things but not enough to actually take action.

I know many people who have attended numerous "Wealth Creation Seminars." You know the ones. They claim to be run by people who only a couple of short years ago were destitute, homeless, and living on the street eating out of bins. And now, today, they're financially free, own half the civilized world, and are competing with Warren Buffet and Bill Gates for the title of world's richest individual.

Don't get me wrong. The information that they give out on most of these seminars will increase your wealth . . . if you take action! And that's the point. People's passion, people's "want to," runs out often when the hard yards start, when you have to back your own judgment.

And so we hear things like "I will invest in property one day. But not just yet. The market is over-inflated." Or "Never again. I bought a property once and let me tell you how I got ripped off and how the tenants ruined my investment" Or "I will buy some shares in about another 6 months. I think the market is headed for a correction and I want to buy at the bottom." Or "I want to buy some shares but I need to do some more research on the companies before I actually take the plunge."

And so those people obviously do not "want to" enough.

We have already looked at this in previous chapters. We called it Commitment.

How to . . . the Plan

Even if you have bucket loads of passion, by itself it will get you into trouble. Let's say that you needed heart surgery tomorrow. Would you hand the scalpel to your partner or parent? Unless they are an open heart surgeon, the answer is probably a resounding no.

They might want to see you well. They might want to see you well with a passion. Sadly they are missing the "how to," plan.

In order to produce exceptional results, you will need a degree of knowledge, skill, and expertise. In previous chapters this was referred to as Competence.

Chance to . . . the Resources

I was a participant in a training program run by one of Australia's best corporate trainers, Colin James. As well as being an exceptional trainer, he is also an accomplished artist. He would be able to pick someone out of the audience and, Rolf Harris like, draw a caricature of them that was instantly recognizable to others in the room. Very clever.

After sitting in on one of his programs, I said to him that I really admired his drawing ability and that I had always wanted to draw like that.

Colin said "No you haven't Rod."

"What do you mean?" I asked.

"You have not always wanted to draw like that." He started. "If you really wanted to draw like that, you would have enrolled yourself in an Art class at your local community TAFE and then you would have bought paper and textas and you would have set aside 3 hours a night 3 nights a week to practice. If you did all that you would be able to draw every bit as good as me."

It's true. The TAFE course is of course the "how to," the "want to" was not sufficient to take action, and the "chance to" was the resources. The time, the textas, the paper.

As discussed in the beginning of this book, it is your role as a manager to be a provider of resources to your team. To ensure that they have sufficient time, equipment, budget, and support to produce the results you ask of them.

So we have already talked about the above issues earlier in the book. One that we have not yet discussed is . . .

Clarity of Purpose . . . the Direction

Significant vision always precedes significant results. There are many examples of this. A man by the name of Viktor Frankel writes of his experiences in Nazi concentration camps during World War II in a book entitled *Man's Search for Meaning*. It is an awesome work that then goes on to establish a form of psychotherapy called "Logotherapy."

What he noticed through his experiences both in the concentration camps and his experience as a psychologist is that the people who survive great stress and tragedy in their lives, the people who have left a mark on this earth, the people who have achieved great things, are not necessarily the strong, the rich, or even the most fit. They are those who have something significant yet to do. They are not ready to die, they are not ready to give in, they have not completed "their mission here on earth" or the raison d'être.

Purpose is powerful.

If you look at a 25-watt light bulb, you would not do any real damage to your eye. If you look into a 25-watt laser beam, you could blind yourself. Why? What is the difference? Both are driven by only 25 watts of power!

The difference is, of course, that the laser beam is concentrated energy. It is focused on one point, while the light bulb has its energy heading off in 360°.

How many team members do you have that seem to be working to their maximum capacity and yet returning minimum results? This could be due to a lack of focus.

An exceptional manager will link activities to the big picture without micro-managing. They will identify principles and values to work by without dictating standards. They will provide direction for their team members without telling them what to do.

When this is done well, it results in a team member who has the focus of a laser beam combined with the passion derived from ownership and empowerment.

On a Number of Levels

It is worth thinking about this on a number of levels.

1. Your team. Your role as a manager, as discussed, is to ensure that your team members have the clarity of purpose, competence, commitment, and resources to complete the work required.

2. You as a manager/leader. If you want to be considered an exceptional manager, then here's what you need to do . . . Clarify what you consider to be an exceptional manager, gain some competence, commit to doing whatever it takes, and then provide yourself with the time, budget, equipment, and support required.

3. Your organization. In order for your organization to achieve exceptional results, the same rules apply. Your role within that is to take the organization's purpose and translate it into purpose for yourself and your team members.

Linking into Your Organizations Purpose

The difficulty with linking into your organization's purpose is that it often exists in a different language from plain English.

- Strategic plans
- Intention Statements
- Vision
- Mission
- Values
- Balanced Score Cards.

The information that you need is there, the skill is in translating them into something that will fire up the individuals in your team.

When you are working for the weekend, or working at a level in the organization that is miles from the rarefied, thinner air of senior management it is very difficult to get excited about profitability, return to shareholders, efficiencies, mergers, and acquisitions. This is management speak, not team members speak.

How do you translate it into something that will motivate, inform, empower, and prepare?

Easy . . .

You structure your message using a process we learnt when talking about coaching.

- Answering the "Why" question using our what's in it for me (WIIFM) motivates
- Answering the "What" question using the Concept/Principles/ Details process informs
- Answering the "How" question using their involvement empowers
- Answering the "What else/what if" question prepares.

Formatting Your Direction Setting Meeting

Imagine that it is the beginning of your appraisal year, the beginning of the calendar year, the beginning of the financial year, the beginning of a project or whenever you reset goals and direction for your team.

Set a team meeting. The aim of the meeting is to establish direction for the coming period and determine a plan to make it happen.

Using the approach suggested as a basis for that meeting, the meeting might sound like the following.

Why

As you know, we are about to start a new period/project. I was thinking about last period/project and noticed that there were some times that we were very stressed and frustrated with things, we also made some mistakes that we might have been able to avoid and I think most of us would agree that we spent more time at work than was necessary.

So what I would like to do today is to spend some time looking at our aims for the coming period/project and determine what we can do to:

- Reduce the stress and frustration potentially associated with the upcoming period/project.
- Increase the likelihood we get things right first time.
- Maintain our sanity and a healthy sense of balance between work and home.

What

The goals of this period/project are primarily around efficiency and value.

The specific goals that have been set for us this year are:

- To reduce our processing error rate to below X percent within the period.
- To improve the level of service as measured by our customer survey to an average response of 7/10 by the next survey.
- To increase profit either through reducing costs or increasing revenue by 3 percent by the end of the period/project.

How

Now, I know that there will be some concerns, challenges, issues, and also some obvious places to start. I want to hear from everyone.

I propose a three-step process for this meeting:

1. Build as big a list of ideas as to what we can do to achieve these targets as we can.
2. Identify the best ideas.
3. Build a plan to implement the best ideas.

And if we keep to time, we should come out of this meeting with a clear direction for the coming period/project.

In order to make sure that this planning time is as efficient as possible, I would like to set a couple of ground rules:

1. Please talk about what we can do, not what we can't do. If you have a concern about an idea that someone has tabled, then please start with the phrase "If we do that we will also need to . . ." rather than the phrase "No we can't do that because . . ."
2. All ideas must be gathered before we judge them. If we are going to reach these targets, we will need a big list of ideas to choose from first and then critique the best ideas.
3. Please be responsible for ensuring that everyone has a fair say, particularly when their area of expertise is being discussed.

OK. So rather than me telling you, you are the experts in all of this. What can we do as a team to achieve these goals?

(Build list, judge best ideas, and the build action plan)

What Else/What If

Well I would just like to thank and congratulate the team for your skill and effort in developing this plan. I think that this plan is about as good as it could be without the benefit of hindsight.

What I'd like us to do now is to spend a bit of time applying the benefit of hindsight to this plan as much as we can.

The way we can do this is to apply some scenarios to the plan and use those scenarios to begin to develop some early warning systems that our plan could be going off the rails and some tactics that will help us get the plan back on track.

So, with this in mind, let's answer these questions and if you can add any other scenarios, please let us know so we can deal with them as well.

- Question 1. What would happen if the market turned against us and revenue dropped? What would be some early warning signals for that scenario and what could we do to bolster our position?
- Question 2. What would happen if the organization was unable to provide us with some of the key resources that we need to pull this off? What would be some early warning signals for that scenario and what could we do to bolster our position?
- Question 3. What would happen if the goal posts were moved mid-year? What would be some early warning signals for that scenario and what could we do to bolster our position?

Thanks again for all you efforts, thought, and input in this meeting. Not only did I learn a lot more than I expected, I also think that we have already headed three possible crises that we might not have even seen coming if we had not have held this meeting.

CHAPTER 9

Don't Be a Turkey

A Little Parable to Finish with

Once upon a time there was a farm. On this farm there were ducks, geese, cows, and a bunch of turkeys. Now, as you may know, the turkey is a grounded bird. They rely on what is on the ground to survive. So every day farmer Jones would come out, throw some seed on the ground, and that is all the turkeys had to survive on until the next day. They had also never gone beyond the confines of the farm fence. So all they ever had experienced about life, the universe, and everything was what existed inside the farm yard. They led a very predictable, dull, and boring experience.

Not far from this farm there was a large mountain range full of canyons and cliffs. At the top of one of the cliffs, there was a nest and the nest belonged to a family of Eagles.

Now I don't know if you have ever seen a free eagle fly, it is a truly phenomenal sight. They are amazing birds. They know exactly the style of clouds that have thermals or updrafts underneath them and they use these thermals to circle higher and higher and higher. They can get to a height that few other birds are able to attain with a minimum of effort.

From that height, they have an eyesight that is many times more powerful than ours. They are able to see a ripple in a pond or a rustle in a bush, know that it means dinner, swoop down, and grab the fish or rabbit out of nowhere. They are amazing birds.

Every day the turkeys used to watch the eagles fly above them, circling to a fantastic height, locating their own food, and being able to meet their needs with far more proficiency, control, excitement, and sense of achievement. The turkeys got to wondering, as turkeys will do: "Imagine if we could fly like that. If we could fly like that, our lives would be far more interesting, exciting, and rewarding."

So a few of the turkeys got together and decided that they would visit the eagles and see if they would teach them how to fly. So off they set. They left the confines of the farmyard and they started walking up the mountains.

At about lunch time, a few of them looked around and could not see any of farmer Jones' seeds. They started to feel very hungry and so they decided that life outside the farm was a little too difficult. They went back to the farm yard and lived the life they had always known. Some continued.

As the sun began to set, the path became difficult to see and the gradient of the climb became much greater. Some of the remaining group felt that it was impossible to get to the top and, even if they did, the eagles would most likely be too busy to teach them how to fly. They went back to the farm yard and lived the life they had always known. Some continued.

Early next morning, after an arduous climb, the remaining turkeys arrived at the eagles nest. They said to the eagles, "We are the turkeys from the farm below and every day we watch you fly high above us. We would like to learn how to fly like you. Please teach us."

The eagles replied that they were happy to teach anyone who was committed. The eagles then started to tell of a process of learning that involved losing feathers, potentially breaking bones, or even critical injury. Some decided that it wasn't that important after all. They went back to the farm yard and lived the life they had always known. Some continued.

At first there were lost feathers, broken bones, and some injuries, but those turkeys who really wanted to fly, persisted with the learning.

After a number of days, the remaining turkeys found that when they jumped from the cliff they were able to miss the ground! They were able to miss the ground for long enough to find a cloud. That certain style of cloud that has updrafts underneath. They also found that by maneuvering their wingtips in a certain fashion they were able to ride the thermal higher and higher and higher. Until they got to a height . . . Wow. What a view. They could see the farm, they could see the hills and valleys beyond the farm, they could even see the curvature of the earth in the distance.

They returned to the eagles ecstatic, exhilarated, and excited. They said to the eagles, "Thank you so much. Our lives have been fundamentally transformed. We will now be able to live a life that is so much more self-sufficient, fulfilling, and meaningful as a result. Once again, thank you!"

The eagles accepted their thanks and bid them a safe journey.

Then the turkeys walked home . . .

They walked home! The dopey birds had just learnt to fly and then they walked home.

Don't be a turkey! You have just invested your valuable time, effort, and money to develop your skills as an exceptional manager. The time to start using this information, these skills, this expertise is not next Monday, not tomorrow . . . it is now. As soon as you close this book and put this book down.

Thank you very much for your commitment to improve the quality of management for your current and future team members.

Fly. Be free.

Bibliography

Block, P. 1996. *Stewardship: Choosing Service over Self-Interest.* Berrett-Koehler; Reprint edition. ISBN: 1881052869

Bolton, R. 1986. *People Skills.* Touchstone Books; Reissue edition. ISBN: 067162248X

Covey, S.R. 1990. *Seven Habits Of Highly Effective People.* Simon & Schuster; 1st edition. ISBN: 0671708635

de Bono, E. 1996. *Edward de Bono's Textbook of Wisdom.* Viking. ISBN: 0670870110

Deep, S., and L. Sussman. 1993. *What to Ask When You Don't Know What to Say. 555 Powerful Questions to Use for Getting Your Way at Work.* Prentice Hall. ISBN: 0139539859

Gerber, M.E. 1995. *The E-Myth: Why Most Businesses Don't Work and What to Do About It.* Harper Business; Updated edition.

Hill, N. 1990. *Think and Grow Rich.* Fawcett Books; Reissue edition. ISBN: 0449214923

Laborde, G.Z. 1987. *Influencing with Integrity Management Skills for Communication & Negotiation.* Syntony Publishing. ISBN: 0933347103

McCarthy, B., S. Leflar, and M.C. McNamara. 1987. *The 4Mat Workbook: Guided Practice in 4Mat Lesson and Unit Planning.* Excel, Incorporated.

Roberts, R., R. Ross, and B. Smith. 1994. *The Fifth Discipline Fieldbook: Strategies and Tools for Building a Learning Organization,* eds., P.M. Senge, and A. Kleiner. Currency/Doubleday. ISBN: 0385472560

Zigarmi, P., D. Zigarmi, K.H. Blanchard. 1999. *Leadership and the One Minute Manager: Increasing Effectiveness Through Situational Leadership.* William Morrow & Co. ISBN: 0688039693

About the Author

Rod Matthews has an international reputation as a leading authority on change and human performance and has unashamedly been described as "the best trainer in Australia." He is skillfully able to engage groups of people and move them from a place of confusion and sometimes even hostility to a place of confidence, clarity, and consensus. Rod delivers on his promise and "gets the message across" by engaging his audience with wit and intelligence and with entertaining, dynamic, and practical training methodologies. Rod works for all organizations across all industries—wherever there are people. For over 20 years, his experience, enthusiasm, and natural curiosity have allowed him to build an encyclopedic knowledge of tips, tools, and techniques that inspire, motivate, inform, and educate. Rod's qualifications include: Graduate Certificate of Study Integrated Human Studies—University of Western Australia; Certificate of Leadership—Cornell University; Certificate of Qualification of Educational Applications of Generative Learning and Neuro-Linguistic Programming; and Graduate Diploma of Adult Education. His accreditations include: The Leadership Circle, Myers–Briggs Type Indicator, and DiSC Profile.

Index

Ability, of team members, 20
  objective analysis of, 21–24
Advertisements, 74
Advertisers, 42
Aggressive counseling, 69
Argument, 84–88
Attitude, of team members, 20
  objective analysis of, 21–24

Behavior Description Generator, 53–54
  to describe performance, 78
  to identify behavior descriptions,
      17–18
Behavior, 14
  descriptions, from value judgments,
      15–19
Billboard, 42
The Blamer, 82
Budgets, 8

Cause identification counseling,
    defined, 69
Centre for Creative Leadership, 25
Coaching, to team members, 31–48
  session, 35–41
    example for, 47–48
Commitment, 100
  ways to improve, 69
Competence, 100
Counseling #1, to stay out of unfair
    dismissal courts, 93
Counseling #2, to stay out of unfair
    dismissal courts, 93
Counseling, team members, 67–90
  aggressive, 69
  asking a question, 81
  conversation, ways to open, 69–77
    possible responses to, 81–82
    principles for dealing with poor
        responses, 82–88
    when to stop, 88–90
  low commitment, causes of, 67–68

observed think feel desire (OFTD),
    77–81
  psychoanalysis, 69
  ways to improve commitment, 69
  works best, 67
Customer Relationship Management
    (CRM) system, 62

Deadlines, 62
Degree of disassociation, 75
The Denial, 82
Desire component, of OFTD, 78,
    80–81
Development, 49–65
  key principles to, 51–52
  plan, 56
    building, 60–62
    example for, 63
    implementing, 64
  process, 52–65
    monitor progress, 65
    needs and wants, identifying,
        54–56
    start with recognition, 52–54
  tactics, identifying, 56–60
Direction, establishing
  clarity of purpose, 101–102
  setting meeting, formatting,
      104–106
  for team members, 99–106
Documented counseling #1, to stay
    out of unfair dismissal courts,
    95–96
Documented counseling #2, to stay out
    of unfair dismissal courts, 96

The E Myth, 7
Eddy system, 46
"EDI" system, 46, 65
80/20 rule, 50
Entrepreneurs, 42
  role of, 10–11

Excellent manager, 2
Exceptional leader, 64
Exceptional manager, 2, 13, 52, 58,
        64, 92, 102–103
    don't be a turkey, 107–109
Exceptional performance,
        components to, 99–102

Feedback
    for improving performance, 45–46
    positive, 73–77
    providing, 52–54
Feeling
    component of OFTD, 77, 80
    versus thinking, 83–84
Ford, Henry, 99
Frankel, Viktor, 101–102

Gerber, Michael E., 7
    three hats of business, 7–11
Good manager, 90, 91
Graham Bell, Alexander, 99

Harris, Rolf, 101
High ability–high attitude, 28
High ability–low attitude, 28
Hill, Napoleon, 99
"How" frame, coaching tool, 40–41,
        47, 103
    for direction setting meeting, 105
Human resources department, 6

Insanity, defined, 31

James, Colin, 101
The Justification, 82

Knowledge, 20
Kolb, David A., 36
Kolbe, Kathy, 36

Labels, to describe performance,
        14–15
Law of reciprocity, 50
Leadership
    flexibility, increasing, 25–26
    style of, 26
    tactic grid, 27–29

Learning styles, 36
Logical levels
    as guide to construct message
        concept, 33, 47
        details, 34–35, 47
        principles, 33–34, 47
Logotherapy, 101
Low ability–high attitude, 27–28
Low ability–low attitude, 28–29
Low commitment, 88–89

Management
    key components of, 8–9
    lessons, 4–7
    speak, 103
Manager
    aim of, 10
    role of, 8
Man's Search for Meaning, 101
Marketers, 42
McCarthy, Bernice, 36
Milestones, 62
Multiple contexts, 56

Observed component, of OFTD,
        77–79
Observed think feel desire (OFTD),
        77–81
Oral warning, 94–95
Organizational resources, affecting
        performance, 21
Organizations purpose, linking team
        members into, 103
Out of the Front Door (OTFD),
        77–81

Pace before you lead an argument,
        84–88
Passion, 99–100
People, 9
Performance analysis, of team
        members, 13–24
Performance appraisal system, 93
    criticism of, 13
Performance improvement
    balanced feedback, providing,
        45–46
    developing, 49–65

tactics to, 25–29
of team members, 1–2
analyzing, 13–24
don't be turkey, 107–109
in workplace, 14–15
Personal development, 58–60
Poor coaching, 44
Poor manager, 45, 90
Pre-framing, 55–56
practice, 44–45, 48
Principles for dealing with poor
responses, 82–88
Professional development, 57
tactics, 57–58
Psychoanalysis counseling, 69

The Quitter, 82

Reassigning, team members, 91–97
Recognizing people, 51, 52–54
Resources
affecting performance, 20–21
to team members, 101
Responses
to conversation, 81–82
poor, principles for dealing with,
82–88
Rewarding people, 51
Rightsizing, 88–89
Rockefeller, John D., 99

Sacking, alternatives to, 91
Services, termination of, 96
SMART goals, 60–62
Stretching people, 51–52
Subjectivity, issue of, 13–15
"Super Technician", 9–10
Systems, 8–9

TAFE course, 101
Team members
coaching to, 31–48
counseling, 67–90

developing, 49–65
direction setting meeting for,
104–106
establishing direction for, 99–106
linking into organizations
purpose, 103
performance improvement of,
analyzing, 13–24
reassigning, 91–97
resources to, 101
Technician
benefits of, 7
drawbacks of, 7
role of, 8, 9
Termination of services, 96
Think and Grow Rich, 99
Thinking
component of OFTD, 77, 79–80
versus feeling, 83–84
on number of levels, 102–103
Three hats of business, 7–11
Training course, 31–32
Turkeys, 107–109

Unfair dismissal courts, ways to stay
out of, 93–96

Value judgments, to behavior
descriptions, moving, 15–19

Wealth Creation Seminars, 100
"What else/what if" frame, coaching
tool, 41, 48, 103
for direction setting meeting,
105–106
"What" frame, coaching tool, 37–39,
40, 47, 103
for direction setting meeting, 104
"Why" frame, coaching tool, 37–39,
41–44, 47, 103
for direction setting meeting, 104
Workplace, performance
improvement in, 14–15

OTHER TITLES IN THE HUMAN RESOURCE MANAGEMENT AND ORGANIZATIONAL BEHAVIOR COLLECTION

- *The 360 Degree CEO: Generating Profits While Leading and Living with Passion and Principles* by Lorraine A. Moore
- *Organizational Design in Business: A New Alternative for a Complex World* by Carrie Foster
- *Power Quotes: For Life, Business, and Leadership* by Danai Krokou
- *Magnificent Leadership: Transform Uncertainty, Transcend Circumstance, Claim the Future* by Sarah Levitt
- *Negotiating with Winning Words: Dialogue and Skills to Help You Come Out Ahead in Any Business Negotiation* by Michael Schatzki
- *Conflict First Aid: How to Stop Personality Clashes and Disputes from Damaging You or Your Organization* by Nancy Radford
- *Temperatism, Volume I: A New Way to Think About Business and Doing Good* by Carrie Foster
- *The Challenge to Be and Not to Do: How to Manage Your Career and Maximize Your Potential* by Carrie Foster
- *Slow Down to Speed Up: Lead, Succeed, and Thrive in a 24/7 World* by Liz Bywater
- *The Illusion of Inclusion: Global Inclusion, Unconscious Bias, and the Bottom Line* by Helen Turnbull
- *On All Cylinders: The Entrepreneur's Handbook* by Ron Robinson
- *Employee LEAPS: Leveraging Engagement by Applying Positive Strategies* by Kevin E. Phillips
- *Making Human Resource Technology Decisions: A Strategic Perspective* by Janet H. Marler and Sandra L. Fisher
- *Feet to the Fire: How to Exemplify And Create The Accountability That CreatesGreat Companies* by Lorraine A. Moore
- *HR Analytics and Innovations in Workforce Planning* by Tony Miller

Announcing the Business Expert Press Digital Library

Concise e-books business students need for classroom and research

This book can also be purchased in an e-book collection by your library as

- *a one-time purchase,*
- *that is owned forever,*
- *allows for simultaneous readers,*
- *has no restrictions on printing, and*
- *can be downloaded as PDFs from within the library community.*

Our digital library collections are a great solution to beat the rising cost of textbooks. E-books can be loaded into their course management systems or onto students' e-book readers.
The **Business Expert Press** digital libraries are very affordable, with no obligation to buy in future years. For more information, please visit **www.businessexpertpress.com/librarians**. To set up a trial in the United States, please email **sales@businessexpertpress.com**.

www.ingramcontent.com/pod-product-compliance
Lightning Source LLC
Chambersburg PA
CBHW062035200326
41519CB00017B/5042